THE BRESLOV SONGBOOK
VOLUME 3

במוצאי יום מנוחה
B'Moitso'ei Yoim M'nuchoh

ניגוני חסידי ברסלב

מוצאי שבת

REBBE NACHMAN'S SONGS

THE TRADITIONAL MUSIC OF CHASSIDEI BRESLOV
FOR MOITSO'EI SHABBOS

Collected and transcribed by
Ben Zion Solomon

Published by
BRESLOV RESEARCH INSTITUTE
JERUSALEM / NEW YORK

First Edition

Cover Photo and Design: Ben Zion Solomon

For further information

Breslov Research Institute

POB 5370 Jerusalem, Israel

Tel.: 972.2.582.4641

Fax: 972.2.582.5542

www.breslov.org

North America:

POB 11, Lakewood, NJ 08701

 or

POB 587 Monsey, NY 10952-0587

Tel.: 732.534.7263/ 1-800-33 BRESLOV

Fax: 732.608.8461

South America:

Guillermo Beilinson

Calle 493 Bis #2548

Gonnet 1897 Argentina

This volume is dedicated to the memory

of my beloved mother

פֵּיגאַ בת יהודא

Florence Solomon

whose unconditional love, encouragement and inspiration

has propelled and guided me through life,

in the spirit of the exemplary Jewish mother

B.Z.S.

PUBLISHER'S PREFACE

"A person should always set his table at the end of Shabbat, even if he can only eat a little" (*Shabbos* 119b).

Rashi explains the importance of the Melave Malka meal after Shabbat as a sign of respect. We set our table and honor Shabbat as it departs, much as one would honor and accompany a king when he arrives in the city (as we do on Shabbat eve) and when he leaves the city.

This is the reason for the "Fourth Meal" of Shabbat. We are commanded to eat three meals on Shabbat; the *Melave Malka* (literally, "Accompanying the Queen") is known as the Fourth Meal. Halakhically speaking, one should eat bread at this meal, but if he is too full from his Shabbat meals, he can suffice with a piece of cake or even a fruit (Mishneh Berurah 300:1).

Additionally, we find that the three meals of Shabbat correspond to the Three Patriarchs, Abraham, Isaac and Jacob, and are metaphorically said to parallel a three-legged table or a three-legged chair. The Fourth Meal is said to parallel King David, who represents the fourth leg, making the table stand secure on its legs.

As we find with Shabbat, many composers established table songs (*zmiros*) and melodies (*niggunim*) to honor the Shabbat Queen as it departs. These poems and songs can be found in many *siddurim* (prayer books). The musical tradition of Breslov Chassidut features many beautiful and soul-stirring renditions of these poems and songs as a tribute to King David, the "Sweet Singer of Israel" (II Samuel 23:1).

Since the time of Rebbe Nachman, Breslover Chassidim often gather together to sing these songs at the *Melave Malka*. In this volume, we have arranged the zemirot with melody and chords to enable anyone who can play an instrument to learn these wonderful tunes. Their delight and depth, their titillating expressions and their intoxicating thrill are credited with drawing people closer to God.

The Breslov Research Institute congratulates Benzion Solomon for yet another incredible achievement, arranging, scoring and recording these classic Breslov melodies to preserve them for eternity. May HaShem bless him and his family with everything good, in this world and the Next. Amen.

Chaim Kramer

Kislev 5773 / November 2012

PREFACE

Rebbe Nachman of Breslov relates in *Likutey Moharan* I, Lesson 117 that people find it difficult to sleep on Moitso'ei Shabbos because at this time there occurs a powerful revelation of Eliyohu HaNovi (Elijah the prophet), who is tasked with heralding the coming of Moshiach and answering all the difficult and as yet unanswered questions — i.e. the establishing of truth and the eliminating of falsehood. The Rebbe teaches that since the origin of untruth — the Serpent in the primordial garden — is the cause of death, and sleep is said to be one-sixtieth of death (*Berochos* 57b), the presence of Eliyohu with his remedy for falsehood/death pushes off sleep. This revelation of Eliyohu is especially strong due to the fact that for the two days previous (i.e., Friday and Shabbos), he cannot come (see *Eruvin* 43b). The build-up of longing causes a restlessness that manifests in increased sleeplessness and the need to go out, often to sing and dance.

Just as we sing *zmiros* to escort the Shabbos as it enters, we also do so as it departs - as one would escort a king's arrival and departure. In this spirit, many of Israel's greatest poets composed songs for the *Melave Malka* meal, which is held as Shabbos leaves and blends into the new week. Many of the beautiful songs for *Moitso'ei Shabbos* relate to Eliyohu and his assigned tasks. The meal at this occasion is even called the "Fourth Meal of Shabbos." It is brought down in *Likutey Moharan* II, Lesson 104 that Rebbe Nachman was particularly emphatic about singing through the entire order of *zmiros* on Shabbos, including the "Fourth Meal." The melodies sung at the Breslover *Melave Malka* table are treasures of stirring beauty and soulfulness.

This volume serves as a companion to the recording released by the Breslov Research Institute, "*B'Moitso'ei Yoim M'nuchoh*: Rebbe Nachman's Songs, Shabbos 5."

May we be blessed to spend our sleepless nights of *Moitso'ei Shabbos* singing these melodies and bringing great *nachas* to God; and may this speed the arrival of *Moshiach tsidkeinu* and *binyan beis hamikdash, omein v'omein.*

פתח דבר

רבי נחמן מברסלב אומר בליקוטי מוהר"ן ח"א תורה קיז, שהטעם לכך שקשה לבני-אדם לישון במוצאי שבת הוא שבשעה זו מתרחש גילוי מופלא של אליהו הנביא, שתפקידו לבשר לנו על ביאת המשיח ולתרץ את כל הקושיות והשאלות שטרם נענו – כלומר, להעמיד את האמת על מכונה ולבטל את השקר. רבנו מלמד שהנחש הקדמוני בגן-עדן הוא המקור לכל שקר, והוא הגורם גם למוות, ושינה היא אחד משישים במיתה (ברכות נז, ב). לכן נוכחותו של אליהו הנביא ושל יכולתו המיוחדת לתקן את השקר, המיתה, דוחה את השינה. כוחה המיוחד של התגלות זו של אליהו נובע מכך שבשני הימים הקודמים הוא אינו יכול לבוא (ראה עירובין מג, ב). הגעגועים המתעצמים במהלך יומיים אלה גורמים לחוסר מנוחה, המתבטא בקושי לישון ובצורך לצאת החוצה, ולעתים קרובות לשיר ולרקוד.

כשם שאנו שרים זמירות כדי ללוות את השבת בבואה, כן נוהגים אנו בצאתה, כאדם המלווה את המלך בבואו ובצאתו. ברוח זו חיברו רבים מגדולי הפייטנים פיוטים לסעודת מלווה מלכה, המושרים בשעה שהשבת נמוגה אל השבוע החדש. רבים מהפיוטים היפים למוצאי שבת מדברים על אליהו הנביא ומשימתו המיוחדת. הסעודה הזו קרויה לעתים קרובות "סעודה רביעית של שבת". מובא בליקוטי מוהר"ן ח"ב תורה קד שרבי נחמן חיבב במיוחד את שירת כל זמירות שבת כסדרן, כולל ב"סעודה רביעית". המנגינות של ברסלב לפיוטי מוצאי שבת הן אוצר של יופי מרגש ומלא נשמה. באוסף שלפנינו, ניסינו לכלול את סדר הפיוטים השלם בנוסחים העיקריים.

הזמירות הכתובים בספר זה הוקלטו בדיסק בשם "במוצאי יום מנוחה," שאפשר להשיג ממכון נחלת צבי.

יהי רצון שנזכה לבלות את לילות מוצאי השבת חסרי השינה שלנו בשירת ניגונים אלה, ושנעשה נחת רוח ליוצרנו; ויהי רצון שבזכות זה נחיש את ביאת משיח צדקנו וייבנה בית המקדש, אמן ואמן.

ACKNOWLEDGMENTS

Many people have contributed their talents and knowledge to make possible the series on Breslov Music in general, and the present volume in particular. First and foremost is Chaim Kramer, Director of the Breslov Research Institute. He was among those who conceived of the project, and has untiringly persevered to bring it to fruition in accordance with the Institute's dedication to making the teachings of Rebbe Nachman of Breslov, and his followers, readily available to the Jewish world. His scholarly notes served as a basis for much of the biographical material in the book, and his excellent leadership continues to inspire all who work with him.

Next, I must thank all the Breslover chassidim whom I consulted to establish the extent of the repertoire, and to document its music and accompanying data. The list is too long to print in its entirety, but particularly outstanding have been the contributions of Rabbi Nachman Burstein and Rabbi Moshe Bienenstock, who sat with me for hours on end to document the material and filter out all but the authentic elements. Their vast experience and intimate association with the most learned and musical leaders among the elders of the Breslover community, past and present, have made them, so to speak, the ministers of the treasury. My great appreciation is also extended to Rabbi Gedaliah Fleer for providing me with access to his musical source-tapes of Breslover authorities who passed away before this project was conceived. His foresight in recording the songs, and his cooperation in relating his personal experiences with their singers and composers, has made a significant contribution to this work.

Ben Zion Solomon

TABLE OF CONTENTS

התוכן

INTRODUCTION

Before we begin looking at the music and information surrounding it, certain background information is essential in order to place the music in the proper context. In this introduction, we would like to present the reader with some of the more important concepts pertaining to this special musical repertoire.

REBBE NACHMAN OF BRESLOV

For those unfamiliar with the life and teachings of the great *tzaddik*, Jewish leader, teacher and writer, Rebbe Nachman of Breslov, we strongly recommend reading the original Hebrew versions of his works and those of his main disciple, Reb Noson of Breslov. Those for whom the Hebrew language presents an obstacle are referred to the publications of the Breslov Research Institute, which are available in English, Spanish and Russian, and particularly to *Crossing the Narrow Bridge*, a practical guide to Rebbe Nachman's teachings; *Until the Mashiach*, the annotated chronology of Rebbe Nachman's life; *Tzaddik*, the English translation of Reb Noson's biography and commentary on the life of his rebbe; and *Rabbi Nachman's Wisdom*, including his shorter teachings and a compendium of information about Rebbe Nachman's life.

Rebbe Nachman was born in 1772 in the Ukrainian village of Medzeboz. A great-grandson of Rabbi Israel Baal Shem Tov, founder of the Chassidic movement, Rebbe Nachman attained outstanding levels of saintliness and wisdom from a young age. He taught honesty, simplicity and faith. He wove wondrous tales of princesses, giants, beggars and emperors. Rebbe Nachman attracted a devoted following that looked to him as "the Rebbe," their prime source of spiritual guidance and support. After his passing in 1810, Rebbe Nachman's influence remained potent. His teachings spread and his following grew; today, the movement that he initiated is still vibrant and growing. Rebbe Nachman's supreme optimism and down-to-earth wisdom have made him one of the most oft-quoted and studied Jewish teachers of all time.

BRESLOV SHABBOS MUSIC

Rebbe Nachman advised his chassidim to get into the habit of always singing a song. With this in mind, we can begin to anticipate the emphatic depth of spirituality and beauty contained in the Breslover Shabbos *niggunim*. In fact, of the precious few remaining *niggunim* that are attributed undisputedly to Rebbe Nachman, almost all are specifically for Shabbos. Shabbos is the day of the soul, and song is the vehicle for the soul's expression. To experience this, one need only drop in at any Breslover minyan on Shabbos. Throughout the week, after every prayer service, the participants join hands in a circle and dance. On Shabbos, this dance can reach the limits of Jewish spiritual joy. As we hinted in the Preface, the *Melave Malka* (Fourth Meal) is considered part of Shabbos, and the spirit of the *zmiros* for this occasion differ only in that musical instruments may accompany the singing.

> *"The Rebbe told us to sing many zmiros and other Shabbos songs. He said: Do not pay attention to any obstacles...strengthen yourself and sing with joy...the main thing is Sabbath joy."*
>
> *(Rabbi Nachman's Wisdom #155)*

Tonality and Harmony

The tonal and harmonic content of the Breslover repertoire, like that of most 18th-to 20th-century European Jewish Music, combines the tonal and harmonic aspects of all Western music of that period, with the timeless tonal and harmonic uniqueness that characterizes Jewish Music. In most 18th-and-19th-century music, tonality is expressed as the major or minor quality of the music. But in Jewish Music, there are many melodic modes expressing many different intervalic relationships, which in turn express many subtle flavors of emotional content. The usual major and minor modes are just two of the many possibilities of tonal expression. Indeed, it is not at all uncommon to find several modes alternating within a single melody.

This being the third volume in the series on Breslov Music, we refer the reader to the first two volumes: Vol. 1, "Azamer BiSh'vochin," and Vol. 2, "Assader LiS'udoso," where there is a more extensive treatment of some of these topics in the Introduction, Foreword and Appendices.

FOREWORD

We offer here a description of the musical and textual conventions adopted in this series to aid the reader in accurate performance and understanding of this corpus of music.

It should be emphasized that we are dealing with an oral tradition of over two hundred years, passed down from father to son and teacher to student. In most cases, the musical material demands animation that can be achieved only through ornamentation and emphasis that are at the subjective discretion of the singer or player of the music. Thus, "accuracy" is a very relative term, and while accuracy is certainly one of our chief concerns in this series, it must be understood that a fair degree of flexibility must be left to the musician, especially in the dance tunes and table *niggunim* that comprise so much of the repertoire. Even when many of the mainstream Breslover chassidim live in the land of Israel within a geographical radius of less than 60 miles (96 kilometers), the variations encountered in the performance of any given *niggun* are indeed many. However, where the *niggun* is of primary importance, such as those pieces attributed to the more important leaders of Breslov or to the Rebbe himself, we discern a reverence and care in transmitting the music that goes beyond the notes to include even the *t'nuos*, or ornamental nuances of performance.

In our transcriptions, we have tried to convey the simple body of the tune, leaving the animation to the individual musician, with a suggestion to keep it within the bounds of the idiom for the particular genre. On the other hand, where a priority for strict adherence to tradition reaches even to the ornamentation, such as the *niggunim* of the Rebbe, we have tried to indicate nuances and variants of reputable origin.

The melodies are notated in treble clef to make them more accessible, since more people read this clef. It is not a comment on the true range of the melodies. The keys chosen are also not rigid; the reader is advised to transpose them to any comfortable key. Tempo indications are not to be taken too literally, since there may be a range of performance tempi acceptable within the Breslover community; they are merely an approximation of the most common performance tempi.

The large stylized letters: ❶, ❷, ❸, etc. in the music or commentary, indicate the beginnings of unique musical sections in the form. They are used both to help the reader understand the musical form, and to facilitate matching up the text with the music in cases where there are more verses than have been placed under the staff. We have placed indications of chordal harmonies above the melody lines in order to make the music more palatable to the amateur performer who may not be able to harmonize the pieces himself, but who plays guitar, keyboard or some other instrument of harmonic accompaniment. However, it is important to understand, firstly, that the harmonies are not to be construed as authoritative or necessary, and, secondly, that the music is purely vocal music, as instruments are never used on Shabbos. But it is not uncommon to find, among the more musically sophisticated Breslovers, a harmony line being sung to a *niggun* either during the dancing at the synagogue, or the meal at home. Most of the harmonies provided here match those employed in the recordings released by the Breslov Research Institute.

The original Hebrew text for each song has been provided along with an English translation and transliteration. The translation emphasizes the literal rather than the poetic content of the original Hebrew text.

A brief comment is offered here on the method of transliteration. While today there are many

Breslovers who come from a Sefardic or even Yemenite background, by and large the community is and has been made up of Eastern European Jews, whose mother tongue was Yiddish, and who pronounced the Hebrew language in the Ashkenazic tradition. Therefore, it was decided in the interest of authenticity to preserve this pronunciation in the transliteration. There is also an inherent accent pattern found in this dialect that has often been included here, even though it is recognized as breaking the rules of Hebrew grammar, to render a more authentic quality to the songs. We have used the following criteria for transliteration:

There has been no differentiation in the transliteration of the Hebrew letters "chaf", כ, and "ches", ח, both being rendered "ch."

Likewise, there has been no differentiation in the transliteration of the Hebrew letters "kaf", כ, and "kuf", ק, both being rendered "k."

The letter "ayin," ע, has most often been rendered as an inverted apostrophe, ʻ, preceding the transliteration of the vowel sound that accompanies it.

The letter "sav," ת, has been transliterated as "s," while the "tav," ת, is "t."

In certain cases, especially where a particular word is in common usage with its Modern Hebrew pronunciation or transliteration, we have acquiesced to common usage to avoid misunderstanding.

The vowel points, or "nikud," have been transliterated according to the following table. The phonetic symbols indicating pronunciation follow the transliteration in parentheses.

komets	ㅜ	o (ô)
pasach	—	a (ä)
tseirei	··	ei (a)
segol	·.·	e (ε)
chirik	·	i (ê)
sh'vo	:	' (ə)
choilom	וֹ	oi, o
shuruk (kubutz)	וּ ·.·	u (oo)

One inconsistency is the transliteration of the vowel *choilom*, which in Eastern Europe was generally pronounced "oi," as indicated in the preceding table. In modern "*s'faradi*" Hebrew, it is pronounced like the name of the English letter "o." When we are not quoting the Breslover repertoire, we have tried to use the latter, more prevalent, pronunciation, as in "*sholosh s'udos*" instead of "*sholoish s'udois*."

In following this system of transliteration we are not asserting any judgment on the subject, other than one of historical authenticity. However, you may employ any dialect you are comfortable with in performance.

A note is in order concerning the usage of God's Hebrew names. These names have been transliterated, taking into account the prohibition of pronouncing God's names if not praying or learning Torah. Thus, the Hebrew letters "heih," ה, (ordinarily transliterated as "h"), "alef," א, (transliterated according to the vowel points associated with it), and "yud", י, (normally, "y") in these names have been replaced by a letter "k." Thus, we find the name "Eloikim" (where the "k" replaces an "h"), the name "Keil" (where "k" joins with the vowel "ei"), and "Koh" (where "k" replaces "y"). The word "HaShem" (literally, "The Name") is used in three ways. Firstly, it replaces the Tetragrammaton, or ineffable four-letter name of God found in traditional texts as "Yud Keih Vav Keih" (where the "Keih" replaces the Hebrew letter "Heih"). An example of this is found in the *zemer* "*Omar HaShem L'Ya'akoiv*" (No. 10 on page 25). Secondly, it replaces the name spelled "Alef Daled Nun Yud" in traditional texts, pronounced "Adonoy" ("My Lord"). We should add here that these replacements need not be applied when actually singing the *zmiros* at the Shabbos or Moitso'ei Shabbos table. Thirdly, the name HaShem has been used in the commentary to the songs, as a synonym for God.

In the Hebrew text of the songs we have used a double "yud" (יי) in place of the Tetragrammaton. Where a holy name is not in the context of one of the *zmiros* or prayers, as in the song titles and table of contents, we have used a hyphenated version of the name.

All the items relevant to a song are found adjacent to the music. We have likewise made an effort to minimize page turning in the middle of a song; therefore you will find half-empty pages.

For a more elaborate *peirush* (commentary) on the text of the *zmiros* the reader is referred to the Hebrew commentaries of the *Etz Yosef* (עץ יוסף) and the *Iyun T'filoh* (עיון תפילה), published, among other places, in the *Siddur Otsar HaT'filos* (אוצר התפילות).

SONGS FOR MOITSO'EI SHABBOS

1. B'MOITSO'EI YOIM M'NUCHOH

בְּמוֹצָאֵי יוֹם מְנוּחָה

Nusach Yerushalmi

By R' Meir Leib Blecher

Adagio

Dm ... **Gm**

B' - moi - tso - ei yoim m' - nu - choh ham - tsei l' -
Eis doi - dim t' - oi - reir Keil l'ma - leit
Bas Tsi - yoin ha - sh' - chu - loh, a - sher
N'chei `am' - cho k'ov ra - cha - mon, y' - tsaf - ts' - fu
Y'hi ha - choi - desh ha - zeh k'n' vu - as
B' - moi - tso - ei yoim gi - loh, shim' - cho

Gm ... **Dm** ... **Dm** ... **Gm**

`am - cho r' - vo - choh, sh'lach Tish - bi l' - ne'e - no - choh v'-noss -
`am a - sher shoi - eil, r'ois tu - v'cho b' - voi goi - eil la - seh
hi hayoim g' - u - loh m'heiroh tih' - yeh b' - `u - loh b'-eim ha -
`am loi al - mon, d'var Ha-Shem a - sher ne - e - mon, ba - ha -
a - vi choi - zeh, viy' - sho - ma b' - va - yis zeh koil
noi - ro `a - li - loh, sh'lach Tish - bi l'-`am s' - gu - loh, re - vach

Gm ... **Dm** **Gm** **Gm**

yo - goin va'a - no - choh. Yo - a - so l' - cho tsu - ri l' - ka - beitz
p'zu - roh ni - do - choh. K'ro ye - sha l' - `am n'do - voh Keil
bo - nim s'mei - choh. Ma'a - yo - nois a - zai y'zu - vun uf' - duyei Ha -
kim' - cho hav - to - choh. Viy' - di - dim p'leitei che - retz n'gi -
so - soin v' - koil sim - choh. Chazak y' - ma - lei m' - shaloi - sei - nu, A - meitz
so - soin v' - ha - no - choh. Koil tsoho - loh v' - ri - noh s'fo - seinu

F **C** **C** **F** **Gm** **Dm** **Bb** **F**

`am m' - fu - zo - ri, mi - yad goy ach - zo - ri a - sher
do - gul mei - r'vo - voh, y' - hi hash' - vu - oh ha - bo liy' - shu -
Shem oid y' - shu - vun, u - mei ye - sha yi - sh'a - vun v' - ha -
no - som yifts'chu v' - me - retz b'li ts'vo - choh uv' - li fe - retz, ein yoi -
ya'a - seh ba - kosho - sei - nu v' - hu yi - sh'lach b' - ma'asei yo - dei - nu b'ro -
oz t' - ra - nei - noh, ono Ha - Shem hoi - shi'o no, o - no Ha-

Rubato Dm   Gm   A7   *a tempo*   Dm   Gm   A7

1, 2, 3, 4, 5 — *6*

ko - ro - li shu - choh.
oh v' - lir' - vo - choh.
tso - roh nish - ko - choh.
tseis ein ts'vo - choh.
choh v' - ha - ts'lo - choh.

Shem hats - li - choh - no.

1. B'Moitso'ei Yoim M'nuchoh

This is the first in the *seder* of *zmiros* for Moitso'ei Shabbos. The text was composed by Ya'akoiv Manu'i, whose name is signed by the initial letters of verses 2-9.

This *niggun* is one of the treasures of Breslov Music. It was composed by R' Meir Leib Blecher, a *talmid muvhak* of Reb Noson of Breslov, and a composer of some of the best Breslover *niggunim*, including "*Oiz V'Hodor*", which we recorded in the BRI disc "Azamer BiSh'vochin", (BRM D-101), and "*Mah Y'didus*," from "MeEyn Olom HaBo" (BRM D-102)".

We have presented two versions of the music, since they are both prevalent today. The main difference is the form of the music.

The first version, which is most prevalent today, is a two-part *niggun* in minor with 4 6/4 bar phrases in each part. The beginning of the A part spells the tonic triad; then phrases alternate between the subdominant (IV) and the tonic (I). The second part, also with 2 6/4 bar phrases, starts on the subdominant and moves to the mediant (III). The last phrase moves back to the tonic, but ends ambiguously on the fifth, which could be harmonized by either I or V. The two parts are repeated six times to complete the text. Some chassidim sing the A part twice for the last verse. Performed thus, there is more of a final cadence at the end, since the melody goes down to the tonic. The chassidim who sing the last verse as the others: |A|B| leave the ending as more of a request of God than as a statement. There is often a retard at the end of the B part in each verse.

The second version was sung by R' Gedalyahu Aharon Kenig z"l whose family and *talmidim* follow his custom. I did not get to ask him from whom he learned it. When I asked members of his family, they answered, "*Mi ziknei anshei shlomeinu (from elders of our chassidim).*" This version is a three-part *niggun* in which the first part is identical to the first version; the second part is only different in its ending, which omits the retard, leading smoothly into a third part. This C part is quite striking in its form and its mode. It consists of three two-bar phrases instead of two. The first phrase, of two bars, begins in the tonic and moves to the IV. The next phrase begins on the III, then changes the mode of the melody from minor to *ahavah rabbah* (חייג'אז) mode, suggesting the cadence VII minor to I major, but ending back on the VII minor. This phrase is then repeated, ending on the I.

B'Moitso'ei Yoim M'nuchoh

As the day of contentment ends, provide relief for Your people; send [Eliyohu] the Tishbite to the groaning nation, so that despair and worry flee.

It is seemly for You, my Rock, to gather in my scattered people from the hand of a cruel nation that has dug me a pit.

Arouse the time of love, O God, and rescue the people that begs to see Your goodness upon the advent of the redeemer, for the scattered, outcast sheep.

Proclaim salvation for the generous people, O God flanked by myriads of angels; may the coming week be one of salvation and relief.

May the bereaved daughter of Zion, who is now despised, soon be wed and become the joyous mother of children.

The wellsprings will then flow, and the Lord's redeemed will return and draw waters of salvation, their troubles forgotten.

Guide Your people like a compassionate father; the unabandoned nation will sing God's faithful word when You fulfill the promise.

The beloved ones who survived the decree will burst forth with song, for there will be no more trouble, tragedy or mishap.

May this month be like the prophecy of the father of all prophets; may there be heard in this house the sound of joy and the sound of happiness.

May the Strong One fulfill our requests, the Courageous One grant our petition; may He send blessing and success to our undertakings.

As the day of delight ends, Awesome Doer, send the Tishbite to the precious people, and relief, joy, and respite as well.

בְּמוֹצָאֵי יוֹם מְנוּחָה

בְּמוֹצָאֵי יוֹם מְנוּחָה. הַמְצֵא לְעַמְּךָ רְוָחָה. שְׁלַח תִּשְׁבִּי לְנֶאֱנָחָה. וְנָס יָגוֹן וַאֲנָחָה:

יָאֲתָה לְךָ צוּרִי. לְקַבֵּץ עַם מְפוּזָרִי. מִיַּד גּוֹי אַכְזָרִי. אֲשֶׁר כָּרָה לִי שׁוּחָה:

עֵת דּוֹדִים תְּעוֹרֵר אֵל, לְמַלֵּט עַם אֲשֶׁר שׁוֹאֵל, רְאוֹת טוּבְךָ בְּבוֹא גוֹאֵל, לַשֶּׂה פְּזוּרָה נִדָּחָה:

קְרָא יֵשַׁע לְעַם נְדָבָה, אֵל דָּגוּל מֵרְבָבָה, יְהִי הַשָּׁבוּעַ הַבָּא לִישׁוּעָה וְלִרְוָחָה:

בַּת צִיּוֹן הַשְּׁכוּלָה, אֲשֶׁר הִיא הַיּוֹם גְּעוּלָה, מְהֵרָה תִּהְיֶה בְּעוּלָה, בְּאֵם הַבָּנִים שְׂמֵחָה:

מַעְיָנוֹת אֲזַי יִזוּבוּן, וּפְדוּיֵי יי עוֹד יְשׁוּבוּן, וּמֵי יֵשַׁע יִשְׁאָבוּן, וְהַצָּרָה נִשְׁכָּחָה:

נְחֵה עַמְּךָ כְּאָב רַחֲמָן. יְצַפְצְפוּ עַם לֹא אַלְמָן, דְּבַר יי אֲשֶׁר נֶאֱמָן, בַּהֲקִימְךָ הַבְטָחָה:

וִידִידִים פְּלִיטֵי חֶרֶץ, נְגִינָתָם יִפְצְחוּ בְּמֶרֶץ, בְּלִי צְוָחָה וּבְלִי פֶרֶץ, אֵין יוֹצֵאת וְאֵין צְוָחָה:

יְהִי הַחֹדֶשׁ הַזֶּה כִּנְבוּאַת אֲבִי חוֹזֶה, וְיִשָּׁמַע בְּבַיִת זֶה קוֹל שָׂשׂוֹן וְקוֹל שִׂמְחָה:

חָזָק יְמַלֵּא מִשְׁאֲלוֹתֵינוּ, אַמִּיץ יַעֲשֶׂה בַּקָּשָׁתֵינוּ, וְהוּא יִשְׁלַח בְּמַעֲשֵׂה יָדֵינוּ בְּרָכָה וְהַצְלָחָה:

בְּמוֹצָאֵי יוֹם גִּילָה, שִׁמְךָ נוֹרָא עֲלִילָה, שְׁלַח תִּשְׁבִּי לְעַם סְגֻלָּה, רְוַח שָׂשׂוֹן וְהַצָּלָה:

Then our lips will sing, with a bright and cheerful voice, "Please, O Lord, save us now! Please, O Lord, grant us success now!"

קוֹל צָהֳלָה וְרִנָּה, שְׂפָתֵינוּ אָז תְּרַנֵּנָה,
אָנָּא יי הוֹשִׁיעָה נָּא, אָנָּא יי הַצְלִיחָה נָּא:

2. B'MOITSO'EI YOIM M'NUCHOH

בְּמוֹצָאֵי יוֹם מְנוּחָה

Nusach of R' Gedalyohu Aharoin Kenig ז"ל

By R' Meir Leib Blecher

Adagio (A)

Em / Am

B' - moi - tso - ei yoim m' - nu - choh ham - tsei l' -
K'ro ye - sha l' - `am n' - do - voh Keil
N'chei `am - cho k' - ov ra - cha - mon, y'tsaf - ts' - fu
Chazak y' - ma - lei m' - sha - loi - sei - nu, A - meitz

Am / Em / Em / Am

`am - cho r' - vo - choh, sh'lach Tish - bi l' - ne'e - no - choh v' - noss - yo
do - gul mei - r'vo - voh, y'hi ha sh' - vu - oh ha - bo liy' - shu -
`am loi al' - mon, d'var Ha - Shem a - sher ne - e - mon, ba - ha -
ya'a - seh ba - ko - sho - sei - nu v' - hu yi - sh'lach b' - ma`asei yo - dei - nu b'ro -

Am / Em / (B) Am

goin va'a - no - choh. Yo - a - so l' - cho tsu - ri l' - ka - beitz
oh v'lir' - vo - choh. Bas Tsi - yoin hash' - chu - loh, a - sher
kim' - cho hav - to - choh. Viy' - di - dim p'leitei che - retz n' - gi -
choh v' - ha - ts'lo - choh. B'moi - tso - ei yoim gi - loh, shim' - cho

G D / G / G / Am / *rit.* / Em Em

`am m' - fu - zo - ri, mi - yad goy ach - zo - ri a - sher ko - ro li shu - choh. Eis
hi ha - yoim g' - u - loh m' - hei - roh tih' - yeh b' - `u - loh b' - eim ha - bo - nim s'mei - choh. Ma'a -
no - som yifts'chu v' - me - retz b'li ts'vo - choh uv'li fe - retz, ein yoi - tseis v' - ein ts'vo - choh.
noi - ro `a - li - loh, sh'lach Tish - bi l'am s'gu - loh, re - vach so - soin v'ha - no - choh. Koil

6

Verse 1 (staff 9–11): doi – dim t'-oi-reir Keil l'-ma-leit `am a-sher shoi – eil, R'-ois tuv' – cho b' – voi goi – eil l' – seh p' – zu – roh ni – do – choh.

Verse 2 (staff 9–11): yo – nois a-zai y'-zu-vun uf'-du yei Ha-Shem oid y'-shu-vun, – U-mei ye – sha yi – sh'a-vun v'-ha-tso – roh nish – ko – choh

Verse 3 (staff 9–11): Y'hi ha-choi-desh ha-zeh k'n' vu-as a-vi choi-zeh, Viy'- sho – ma b'-vayis zeh koil so – soin v' – koil sim – choh.

Verse 4 (staff 9–11): tsoho-loh v'-ri-noh s'fo-sei-nu oz t'-ra-nei-noh, O-no Ha- Shem hoi – shi'o no, o – no Ha-Shem hats' – li-cho no.

Staff 13:
R'- ois tuv'-cho b'-voi goi-eil l'-seh p'-zu-roh ni-do-choh *D.C.*
U-mei ye – sha yi-sh'a-vun v'-ha-tso-roh nish-ko-choh.
Viy'- sho – ma b'-vayis zeh koil so – soin v'-koil sim-choh.
O-no Ha-Shem hoi-shi'o no, o-no Ha-Shem hats'-li-cho no.

7

3. CHADEISH S'SOINI

חַדֵּשׁ שְׂשׂוֹנִי

Chassidei Breslov

Allegro

Em Am Em Am Em Em Am G D G

Cha-deish s'-soi-ni Keil no v'-ho-vi es Ei-li-yo-hu ha-no-vi,
Koi-nein l'-`am zu tso-ri tsur lach'-voish, Le-chem le'e-choil u-veged lil'-boish,

Em Am Em Am Em Em Am Em D Em

A-meits v'-cha-zeik rif-yoin yo-di, Bo-reich m'-lach-ti v'-chol ma`-bo-di, Goi-
m'san-'ai yeche-zeh yei-reh v'-yei-voish, N'-veih har sei-`ir b'-ko-roiv tich'-boish. S'-

Em Am Em D Am D G Em Am Em D Em Am B7

a-li z'choir `on'-yiy u-m'-ru-di, D'vor'-cho ha-toiv ho-keim l'-`oi-d'-di,
soi-ni yig-dal bi-r'ois s'vi-vi, Es Ei-li-yo-hu ha-no-vi.

Em Am Em D Em D G Em Am Em D Em D Em

Ho-reits u-sh'lach v'-sa-mach l'-vo-vi, Es Ei-li-yo-hu ha-no-vi.
S'soi-ni yig-dal bi-r'ois s'vi-vi, Es Ei-li-yo-hu ha-no-vi.

Em Am Em Em Am Em

Vo-`eid v'-ho-chein dei si-pu-ki, Za-mein m'-zoi-ni v'-le-chem chu-ki,
`A-moin u-Moi'-ov m'hei-roh s'-cha-leh, P'dus'-cho l'-`am-cho m'-hei-roh t'-ga-leh,

Am Am D C Am F D Em

Cha-leiv cheil go-yim chish l'-ho-ni-ki, Tuv'-cho t'-sa-ba` `oi-l'-li v'-yoin'-ki,
Tsi-yoin t'-ma-lei mei-`am ei-leh, Kir'-yas melech rov oz na-`a-leh,

8

25 Em Am Em D Am D G   Em Am Em D Em Am B7

Yo - voi M'-shi - chi l'- `ir moi - sho - vi,   Es Ei - li - yo - hu ha - no - vi.

Sha - kein t'- sha - kein b'- soich `am tsvi,   Es Ei - li - yo - hu ha - no - vi.

29 Em Am Em D Am D G   Em Am Em D Em D Em

Yo - voi M'-shi - chi l'- `ir moi - sho - vi,   Es Ei - li - yo - hu ha - no - vi.

Sha - kein t'- sha - kein b'- soich `am tsvi,   Es Ei - li - yo - hu ha - no - vi.

D.C.

Chadeish S'soini

Please, God, renew my joy and bring Eliyohu the prophet. Strengthen and fortify my weakened hands. Bless my labor and all my undertakings. My Redeemer, remember my poverty and my misery—fulfill Your promises and cheer me. Hurry and send Eliyohu the prophet to gladden my heart.

Arrange and prepare all my needs; prepare my food and portion of bread. Hurry, nourish me from the riches of the nations. Satisfy my children and infants with Your goodness; let my Moshiach come to my capital, with Eliyohu the prophet.

Prepare for this people, my Rock, a salve to dress the wound, bread to eat, and clothing to wear. May my enemies behold, fear, and be shamed. May the dwellings of Mount Seir soon be conquered. My joy shall increase when I see around me Eliyohu the prophet.

Ammon and Moab quickly destroy; Your redemption for Your people speedily reveal. Zion shall be filled with this people; to the city of the great King we shall go up. You shall surely cause to dwell among the beloved people Eliyohu the prophet.

חַדֵּשׁ שְׂשׂוֹנִי

חַדֵּשׁ שְׂשׂוֹנִי אֵל נָא וְהָבִיא אֶת אֵלִיָּהוּ הַנָּבִיא, אַמֵּץ וְחַזֵּק רִפְיוֹן יָדַי, בָּרֵךְ מְלַאכְתִּי וְכָל מַעְבָּדַי גֹּאֲלִי זְכוֹר עָנְיִי וּמְרוּדִי, דְּבָרְךָ הַטּוֹב הָקֵם לְעוֹדְדִי, הָרֵץ וּשְׁלַח וְשַׂמַּח לְבָבִי, אֶת אֵלִיָּהוּ הַנָּבִיא:

וְעֵד וְהָכֵן דֵּי סְפוּקִי, זַמֵּן מְזוֹנִי וְלֶחֶם חֻקִּי, חֵלֶב חֵיל גּוֹיִם חִישׁ לְהָנִיקִי, טוּבְךָ תְּשַׂבַּע עוֹלְלֵי וְיוֹנְקִי, יָבֹא מְשִׁיחִי לְעִיר מוֹשָׁבִי, אֶת אֵלִיָּהוּ הַנָּבִיא:

כּוֹנֵן לְעַם זוּ צֳרִי צוּר לַחֲבוֹשׁ, לֶחֶם לֶאֱכוֹל וּבֶגֶד לִלְבּוֹשׁ, מְשַׂנְאַי יֶחֱזֶה יֵרֵא וְיֵבוֹשׁ, נְוֵה הַר שֵׂעִיר בְּקָרוֹב תִּכְבּוֹשׁ. שְׂשׂוֹנִי יִגְדַּל בִּרְאוֹת סְבִיבִי, אֶת אֵלִיָּהוּ הַנָּבִיא:

עַמּוֹן וּמוֹאָב מְהֵרָה תְכַלֶּה, פְּדוּתְךָ לְעַמְּךָ בְּקָרוֹב תְּגַלֶּה, צִיּוֹן תְּמַלֵּא מֵעַם אֵלֶּה, קִרְיַת מֶלֶךְ רַב אָז נַעֲלֶה, שַׁכֵּן תְּשַׁכֵּן בְּתוֹךְ עַם צְבִי, אֶת אֵלִיָּהוּ הַנָּבִיא:

9

3. Chadeish S'soini

This text was penned by a poet named Shilo (שילא), who modestly concealed his name in the final letters of the first four words of the *zemer*. The rest of the verses' initial letters follow the order of the *alef-beis*. The text is a prayer for the appearance of Elijah the prophet, heralding the coming of *Moshiach,* and we add in requests for our physical needs as well. It was adapted by Breslover chassidim to a dance *niggun* brought from Uman. The same *niggun* is often sung on *Leyl Shabbos* during the dancing at the end of *Ma'ariv.* It was also recorded on the album "Azamer BiSh'vochin" (BRM-D 101 No. 6). Some chassidim sing it for "Yoim zeh m'chubad" at the Shabbos morning meal.

Ogil V'Esmach
אָגִיל וְאֶשְׂמַח

I shall rejoice and be glad within my heart when I see that You fight my battle against my enemies, and will bring a redeemer to Zion. Immediately send Tzemach [the Moshiach]. Eliyohu the prophet and Moshiach the king.

אָגִיל וְאֶשְׂמַח בְּלִבָּבִי, בִּרְאוֹתִי כִּי מֵאוֹיְבִי תָּרִיב רִיבִי, וּלְצִיּוֹן גּוֹאֵל תָּבִיא, אִישׁ צֶמַח תַּצְמִיחַ, אֵלִיָּהוּ הַנָּבִיא וּמֶלֶךְ הַמָּשִׁיחַ:

Therefore dread and fear shall fall on all the nations. Their hearts shall fear when the unique nation arises and is successful in all they do. Eliyohu the prophet and Moshiach the king.

לָכֵן בָּעַמִּים יַחַד, תִּפּוֹל אֵימָה וָפַחַד, לִבָּם יִפְחָד, בְּעֵת יַעֲלֶה גּוֹי אֶחָד, וְאֹרְחוֹתָיו יַצְלִיחַ: אליהו

There will yet come a time that He will arouse Himself to make a great slaughter, from east to west, in Aram and Arabia, to wage war and battle; He shall roar at His enemies. Eliyohu the prophet and Moshiach the king.

עוֹד מִמִּזְרָח לְמַעֲרָב, יֵעוֹר לַעֲשׂוֹת הֶרֶג רָב, בַּאֲרָם וַעֲרָב, לַעֲרוֹךְ מִלְחָמָה וּקְרָב, עַל אוֹיְבָיו יַצְרִיחַ: אליהו

Wicked kings of the earth—Yetur, Nafish, Kedmah, Mishma and Dumah—flee south or west, for you will be driven away by Eliyohu the prophet and Moshiach the king.

זֵדִים מַלְכֵי אֲדָמָה, יְטוּר נָפִישׁ וָקֵדְמָה, מִשְׁמָע וְדוּמָה, נוּסוּ נֶגְבָּה וָיָמָּה, אֲשֶׁר אֶתְכֶם יַבְרִיחַ: אליהו

Rejoice, all travelers, for the Jews have been rejuvenated. His light will shine from the Menorah. On Mount Zion shall blossom Eliyohu the prophet and Moshiach the king.

רָנוּ כָּל עוֹבְרֵי אֹרַח, כִּי הִנֵּה רַעֲנָן אֶזְרָח, אוֹרוֹ זָרַח, קָנֶה כַּפְתּוֹר וָפֶרַח, עַל הַר צִיּוֹן יַפְרִיחַ: אליהו

4. Ogil V'Esmach

The composer of this text was named Elazar (אלעזר) and his name is found in the initial letters of the verses. The *niggun* was originally set to the *piyut* "HaShem Melech, Hashem Moloch" from *Shacharis* of Rosh HaShanah. But like so many of the beautiful *niggunim* for Rosh HaShonoh, it is difficult to accept that they are sung only two days a year. This *niggun* found its way to "Ogil V'Esmach" and sounds quite appropriate for the description of the war accompanying the arrival of Elijah the prophet and *Moshiach.* The austerity of the two-part march in the *ahavah rabbah* (חיג׳אז) mode conveys both the victory over the forces of evil and the joy of the final redemption. The multiple repetitions of the phrase "oiroi zorach" ("his light will shine") convey the blossoming of our spiritual enlightenment at this event and a reference to Rebbe Nachman's statement that his light will shine until the coming of *Moshiach.*

4. OGIL V'ESMACH

אָגִיל וְאֶשְׂמַח

Chassidei Breslov

Moderato Ⓐ

O - gil V'-Es - mach bil - vo-vi, bir' -oi-si ki mei-oi - vi to - riv ri - vi,

u - l'-Tsi - yoin goi - el to - vi, Ish tse - mach tats' - mi - 'ach

E - li-yo-hu ha - no-vi u - me-lech ha-mo - shi - ach.

Ⓑ

Lo - chein bo - `a - mim ya - chad, ti-pol ei - moh vo - fa-chad, li - bom
Oid mi - miz - rach l' - ma`a - rav, Yei-'oir la`a-sois he - reg rov, Ba - A - rom
Zei-dim Zei - dim mal-chei a - do moh, Y'-tur no - fish vo - keid'-moh, Mish'-mo
Ro - nu kol `oiv-rei oi - rach, Ki hi - nei ra`a-non ez - roch, Oi - roi zo-rach

yif - chod b' - eis ya`-leh goy e - chod V' - oir cho - sov yats - li - ach,
va - `a - rov, La`a-roich mil - cho - moh u' - krov, Al oi - vov yats - ri - ach
v' - du - moh, Nu - su neg - boh vo - yo - moh, A - sher es - chem yav - ri - ach
Oi - roi zo - rach... Ko - neh kaf - toir vo - fe - rach, Al Har Tsi - yoin yaf - ri - ach

E - li-yo-hu ha - no - vi u - me-lech ha - mo - shi - ach.

11

Eloikim Yis'odeinu

God will sustain us with blessing for our possessions, and grant us success in all our undertakings. God will sustain us.

On Sunday, as we begin the work week, He will grant us blessing; on Monday, He will grant us good advice. God will sustain us.

On Tuesday, Wednesday and Thursday, our successes will continue, without any setbacks or loss. He will send our redeemer. God will sustain us.

On Friday, prepare the meat for the Shabbos meals, for we will laud and praise Him for all we have. God will sustain us.

Tasty, delicious foods for our extra Shabbos-soul are for Shabbos. Our beds are freshly-made; the Shabbos candles illuminate the night. God will sustain us.

אלקים יסעדנו

אֱלֹהִים יִסְעָדֵנוּ. בְּרָכָה בִּמְאוֹדֵנוּ. וְזֶבֶד טוֹב יִזְבְּדֵנוּ, בְּכָל מִשְׁלַח יָדֵינוּ, אֱלֹהִים יִסְעָדֵנוּ:

בְּיוֹם רִאשׁוֹן לַמְלָאכָה, יְצַו אִתָּנוּ בְּרָכָה, וְיוֹם הַשֵּׁנִי כָּכָה, יַמְתִּיק אֶת סוֹדֵנוּ: אלהים יסעדנו

רַבֵּה צְבָאֵי יִשְׁעִי, בַּשְׁלִישִׁי וּבָרְבִיעִי, בַּחֲמִישִׁי אַךְ לֹא בְעִי, יִשְׁלַח אֶת פּוֹדֵנוּ: אלהים יסעדנו

הָכֵן טְבוֹחַ טֶבַח בְּיוֹם הַשִּׁשִּׁי זֶבַח, קֹדֶשׁ הִלּוּל וָשֶׁבַח, עַל כָּל מַחֲמַדֵּנוּ: אלהים יסעדנו

מַעֲדַנִּים לְנַפְשֵׁנוּ, נִתַּן בְּיוֹם קָדְשֵׁנוּ, וְרַעֲנָנָה עַרְשֵׂנוּ, וְלַיְלָה אוֹר בַּעֲדֵנוּ: אלהים יסעדנו

5. Eloikim Yis'odeinu

The author's name, Avraham (אברהם), is found in the initial letters of the verses. The text describes the typical week ahead and asks God for blessing and redemption. The emphasis by repetition, in the last verse, of the word "v'layloh" (וְלַיְלָה), describing Shabbos night when we have a special holy light, recalls the Breslover's predilection of night as the ideal time to go out to the fields for *hisbodedus*, (meditation).

The melody is a dance *niggun* that was set to this text and that of the next *piyut*, "*Keili Chish*", by the Breslover chasidim in Poland.

5. ELOIKIM YIS`ODEINU

אֱלֹקִים יְסָעֲדֵנוּ

Moderato

Chassidei Breslov

A

Dm Dm D Gm D Cm D D

E - loi-kim yis - `o - dei - nu b' - ro-choh bim' - oi - dei-nu, v'ze-ved toiv yiz -

Gm Eb Gm Cm D

b' - dei-nu b' - chol mish-lach yo - dei-nu, E-loi-kim yis - `o - dei - nu. B' -

B

Gm Eb Gdim7 A7 Cdim D D

yoim ri - shoin li - m'lo-choh, y'tsav `i - to-nu b' - ro-choh, v' - yoim ha - shei - ni

Gm D D7 Gm Cm D

ko - choh, yam' - tik yam' - tik es soi - dei - nu, E-loi-kim yis - `o - dei - nu.

C

Gm Gm Bb Gm6 A7 D Gm D Gm

Ra - beih ts'vo - ei yish - `i, ba - sh'li-shi u - vor' - vi - `i, ba -
Ho - chein t'voi - ach te - vach, b'yoim ha - shi-shi ze - vach,
Ma`a - danim l' - naf' - shei - nu, ni - tan b'yoim kod' - shei-nu,

D Gm D Cm D D D Gm

cha - mi - shi ach loi v' - `i, yish - lach yish - lach
koi - desh hi - lul vo - she-vach `al kol machama - dei - nu
v' - ra`a - no - noh `ar' - sei - nu, v'lay - loh lay - loh

D Gm D Gm Cm Eb Cm D

yish - lach yish - lach es poi - dei - nu E - loi-kim yis - `o - dei - nu.
`al kol macha-ma - dei - nu E - loi-kim yis - `o - dei - nu.
v' - lay - loh oir ba`a - dei - nu, E - loi-kim yis - `o - dei - nu.

D.S.

13

Keili Chish

My God, quickly send my redeemer, Your servant, who will bring me success. God, send the harbinger of good news, Eliyohu the prophet.

The mountains will be so beautiful when the messengers [Eliyohu and Moshiach] of their Creator set foot upon them; so, too, the feet of the harbingers, when they proclaim, "Return, return." *My God, quickly send my redeemer...*

Hide for a moment, while I strike your enemies with every illness and plague on the day of My vengeance. *My God, quickly send my redeemer...*

Your king will come to you; you are utterly beautiful. My beloved faces you—[Eliyohu] of Gilead, the Tishbite. *My God, quickly send my redeemer...*

The lips of the dove [Israel] shall drip honey [sweet words], for the time to grace Zion, the beautiful inheritance, has come. *My God, quickly send my redeemer...*

קלי חיש

אֵלִי חִישׁ גּוֹאֲלִי עַבְדְּךָ יַשְׂכִּילִי, מְבַשֵּׂר טוֹב אֵלִי, אֶת אֵלִיָּהוּ הַנָּבִיא:

נָאווּ עַל הֶהָרִים, שְׁלוּחֵי יוֹצֵר הָרִים, וְרַגְלֵי הַמְבַשְּׂרִים בְּאֶמוֹר שׁוּבִי שׁוּבִי: אֵלִי חִישׁ

חֲבִי כִּמְעַט רֶגַע, כָּל מַחֲלָה וְכָל נֶגַע, אֹיְבַיִךְ אֶפְגַּע יוֹם נָקָם בְּלִבִּי: אֵלִי חִישׁ

מַלְכֵּךְ יָבֹא לָךְ, יָפָה אַתְּ כֻּלָּךְ, וְרַעְיָתִי לְמוּלָךְ, גִּלְעָדִי הַתִּשְׁבִּי: אֵלִי חִישׁ

נֹפֶת תִּטֹּפְנָה, שִׂפְתֵי בְנֵי יוֹנָה, כִּי בָא עֵת לְחֶנְנָה, צִיוֹן נַחֲלַת צְבִי: אֵלִי חִישׁ

6. Keili Chish

The subject of the text is again the role of Eliyohu the prophet as the one who prepares the coming of Moshiach.

The name of the poet, Nachman (נחמן), is found in the initial letters of the verses. Since this is also the name of the Rebbe, the Breslover chassidim put great emphasis on the word *Tsiyoin*, which is how we refer to the grave of the Rebbe. Suddenly the prevalent dance tempo slows and this word is sung with great *d'veikus*.

6. KEILI CHISH

קֵלִי חִישׁ

Chassidei Breslov

Moderato

Kei - li chish goi - a - li `av - d'- cho yas - ki - li, m'va - ser toiv Kei - li es Eli -

yo - hu ha - no - vi. No - vu `al he - ho - rim sh'lu - chei Yoi - tseir Ho - rim,
Mal - keich yo - voi loch, yo - foh at ku - loch,

v' rag - lei ha - m' - vas - rim be' - e - moir shu - vi shu - vi. Kei - li chish goi -
v'ra - `a - yo - si l' - mu - loch, Gil - `o - di Ha - tish - bi. Kei - li chish goi -

a - li. Cha - vi kim - `at re - ga` kol ma - chaloh v'- chol ne - g`a
'a - li. Noi - fes ti - toif - noh, sif - sei v' - nei yoi - noh,

oi - va - yich ef - g`a yoim no - kom b' -
ki vo eis l'- che - n' - noh, Tsi - yoin Tsi - yoin Tsi - yoin Tsi - yoin

li - bi. Kei - li chish goi - a - li, Kei - li chish goi - a - li
Tsi - yoin Tsi - yoin Tsi - yoin nacha - las tsvi.

`av - d'- cho yas - ki - li, m'- va - ser toiv Kei - li es E - li - yo - hu ha - no - vi.

15

7. ADIR OYOIM V'NOIRO

אַדִיר אָיוֹם וְנוֹרָא

Adagio

A-dir o-yoim v'-noi-ro, ba-tsar li l'-cho e-k'ro, Ha-
Tuv-cho to-chish l'-a-me-cho, y'hi o-lei-nu kin'u-me-cho, Ha-
P'-deih `am-cho mei-`a-zim, tsoin'-cho mi-yad goiz'-zim, Ha-

Shem li li li li v'-loi i-ro. G'-
Shem aseih l'ma'an Sh'-me-cho aseih l'-ma'an Sh'-me-cho.
Shem `oi-seh cha-zi-zim, `oi-seh cha-zi-zim.

doir pir-tsas pir-tsas hei-cho-li, do-gul ma-heir cha-
Koi-nein beis m'-choi-ne-cho, l'har-beits boi tsoi-
Ko-reiv keits keits ne-cho-moh, ra-cheim oim loi ru-

chli-li, do-gul ma-heir cha-chli-li, Ha - Shem he-
ne-cho, l'har-beits boi tsoi-ne-cho, Ha - Shem b'-
cho-moh, ra-cheim oim loi ru-cho-moh, Ha - Shem

yeih he-yeih he-yeih oi-zer li. Hein
oir po-ne-cho, b'-oir po-ne-cho. Mi-pachad mi-
Ish mil-cho-moh, Ish mil-cho-moh. Sh'choin

16

Measure 20:
G   D   Em   Bm   G   D   Em   Bm   Bm   Em

hein A-toh sik - vo-si, v'li - y'shu-`os-cho ki - vi - si, Ha-Shem
pa - chad ha-tsi - li, nahalei - ni l'Tsi-yoin koi-desh goi-ro-li, Ha - Shem
sh'choin k'mei-oz b'o-ho-lei-nu, sh'choin k'-mei'oz b'o-ho-lei - nu, to-mid to-mid

Measure 25:
Em   A7   D   G   F#7   **B** D   G

oiz y'shu - `o-si  oiz  y'-shu - `o - si.   Zoch   un' -
sh'ma b'-koi-li, sh'ma b'-koi - li,   S'oid u-s'moich
to - mid to - mid Keil m'-choil'-lei-nu,   lai la lai la lai lai

Measure 29:
D   A   Bm   Em   D   A7   D   Em   D   A7   D

ki cha-pa-yim, choin poir - sei ch'no - fa - yim,   choin poir - sei ch'no -
l'-nim-ho-rim, azoir no es ha-nish-a-rim,   azoir no es ha-nish -
lai lai lai lai lai lai lai la la lai lai,   lai lai lai la la

Measure 33:
Em   D G D A7 Bm Em   Bm Em Bm Em F#aug F#7 Bm

fa - yim, Ha - Shem e - rech a-pa-yim e-rech a-pa-yim.
a - rim, Ha - Shem yoi - tseir ho-rim, yoi-tseir ho - rim.
lai lai, Ha - Shem Mal - kei-nu Hu yoi-shi-ei-nu.

Adir Oyoim V'Noiro

Mighty, Awesome, Fearsome One, in my distress I call out to you; God is with me, I shall not fear.

Mend the breach of my Temple. Your Eminence, hasten the Moshiach's arrival. Lord, be my helper.

You are indeed my hope; Your salvation I await. God is the strength of my deliverance.

אדיר איום ונורא

אַדִּיר אָיוֹם וְנוֹרָא, בַּצַּר לִי לְךָ אֶקְרָא, יי לִי וְלֹא אִירָא:

גְּדוֹר פִּרְצַת הֵיכָלִי, דְּגוּל מַהֵר חַכְלִילִי, יי הֱיֵה עוֹזֵר לִי:

הֵן אַתָּה תִקְוָתִי, וְלִישׁוּעָתְךָ קִוִּיתִי, יי עוֹז יְשׁוּעָתִי:

17

Pure One, Who does no wrong, grace those who spread out their hands [in prayer]; God You are slow to anger.

Quickly bring Your good to Your people; may it be for us as You have spoken. God, do this for Your Name's sake.

Establish Your Temple, within which to repose Your flock, God, by the light of Your countenance.

Save me from fear; lead me to Zion, my holy lot. God, hear my voice.

Sustain and support those who rush [to do mitzvot]. Help, please, those who remain, God, Former of mountains.

Redeem Your people from the insolent, Your flock from the hands of the shearers, God, Former of clouds.

Bring closer the End [of Days], the consolation. Have pity on the unpitied nation, God, the Warrior.

Dwell as in yore in our tent, forever, God, our Creator. God is our King—He will save us.

זַךְ וּנְקִי כַפַּיִם, חֹון פֹּורְשֵׂי כְנָפַיִם, יי אֶרֶךְ אַפַּיִם:

טוּבְךָ תָּחִישׁ לְעַמֶּךָ, יְהִי עָלֵינוּ כְּנָאֲמֶךָ, יי עֲשֵׂה לְמַעַן שְׁמֶךָ:

כֹּונֵן בֵּית מְכֹונֶךָ, לְהַרְבֵּץ בֹּו צֹאנֶךָ, יי בְּאֹור פָּנֶיךָ:

מִפַּחַד לְהַצִּילִי, נַהֲלֵנִי לְצִיֹּון קֹודֶשׁ גֹּורָלִי, יי שְׁמַע בְּקֹולִי:

סְעֹוד וּסְמֹוךְ לַנִּמְהָרִים, עֲזֹור נָא אֶת הַנִּשְׁאָרִים, יי יֹוצֵר הָרִים:

פְּדֵה עַמְּךָ מֵעַזִּים, צֹאנְךָ מִיַּד גֹּוזְזִים, יי עֹשֵׂה חֲזִיזִים:

קָרֵב קֵץ נֶחָמָה, רַחֵם אֹום לֹא רוּחָמָה, יי אִישׁ מִלְחָמָה:

שְׁכֹון כְּמֵאָז בְּאָהֳלֵנוּ, תָּמִיד אֵל מְחֹולְלֵנוּ, יי מַלְכֵּנוּ, הוּא יֹושִׁיעֵנוּ:

7. Adir Oyoim V'Noiro

We do not know the name of the author of this *zemer*, but each verse has three parts. The first two go according to the *alef-beis*, and the third reveals a quality associated with God's four-letter name. The words are not directly related to the subjects of Shabbos or Moitso'ei Shabbos, but rather constitute a powerful prayer for the urgent spiritual and physical needs of the Jewish people.

There is a story about the origin of the *niggun*. Rabbi Avraham Sternhartz said that Reb Moishe Breslover, a *talmid* of Reb Noson, was on a Turkish ship bound for the Land of Israel where he heard the sailors singing this melody. When he was asked to join the singing on Moitso'ei Shabbos, he set it to the words of this *zemer*. Rabbi Levi Yitschok Bender said that the *niggun* was composed by Reb Mendel Litvik, one of the group of Chabad chassidim in the time of the Tsemach Tsedek who became Breslovers. The *niggun* is in minor and in three musical parts per verse for four verses: || A | B | C | B' ||. The climax is reached in the third part with its upward leap and pleading for God to protect us from fear or finally to dwell in our tents, to be imminently present in our lives. This *niggun* is the jewel at the center of the crown of Moitso'ei Shabbos *zmiros*.

Ish Chosid Hoyoh

Once there was a pious man, without food or sustenance. He studied [Torah] in his home [rather than in the study hall] out of shame at having no garment to wear. He was the protector of his worthy wife and five children.

His wife said to him, "We don't have to worry any more; there is no bread to eat, we are naked—we have nothing. You attained Torah because you worked hard at it. What will we eat now?

"Go quickly, as an armed warrior, to the marketplace. Perhaps the Gracious and Merciful One on High will bestow goodness on us in His mercy. [He does] good for those who hope for His shelter, and does the will of those who fear Him."

"You counseled with knowledge and wisdom, but I cannot agree with your advice. My going out will be a shame and a disgrace, with nothing to wear. I have nothing to sell, not even for a penny."

She quickly borrowed from the neighbors nice, appropriate clothing. He dressed and cast his burden upon God Whom he loved. The children murmured a prayer, "May the needy one not return shamed."

He went through the marketplace hopefully, and suddenly Eliyohu the prophet approached him. The harbinger said to him, "I guarantee that today you will become rich. Command me as you wish, for I am your servant.

"Shout, 'Who wishes to purchase an unparalleled slave?!'" The pious Jew thought, how could it be possible that a slave should sell his master? [Eliyohu] gave him some of his wisdom, and he held [Eliyohu] as if he were his master.

A merchant willingly purchased him for 800,000 pieces of gold. He asked [Eliyohu], "What are your skills? Do you have any building experience? Complete a banquet hall and a palace, then you shall be a free man!"

The first day of his employment, [Eliyohu] worked with the laborers. He cried out at

אִישׁ חָסִיד הָיָה, בְּלִי מָזוֹן וּמִחְיָה, בְּבֵיתוֹ עוֹסֵק מַלְבּוּשׁ, וְאֵין בֶּגֶד לִלְבּוֹשׁ, גּוֹנֵן בַּחֲשׁוּבָה אִשָּׁה, וְגַם בְּבָנִים חֲמִשָּׁה:

דִּבְּרָה לוֹ הָאִשָּׁה, יוֹתֵר אֵין לְהִתְיָאֲשָׁה, הֲמִבְּלִי לֶחֶם לֶאֱכוֹל, בְּעֵרוֹם וּבְחוֹסֶר כֹּל, וְתוֹרָה מָצָאתָ כִּי יָגַעְתָּ, מַה נֹּאכַל מֵעַתָּה:

זָהִיר כְּבַר נָשׁוּק, הֲלֹא תֵצֵא לַשּׁוּק, חַנּוּן וְרַחוּם בִּמְרוֹמָיו, אוּלַי יִגְמְלֵנוּ כְּרַחֲמָיו, טוֹב לְקֹוָיו מַחֲסֶה, רְצוֹן יְרֵאָיו יַעֲשֶׂה:

יָעַצְתָּ בְּדַעַת וּבְחָכְמָה, עֲצָתֶךְ בְּלִי לְהַסְכִּימָה, כְּצֵאתִי לָבֹשֶׁת וְלִכְלִמָּה, מִבְּלִי כְסוּת וְשַׂלְמָה, לְאֵין בְּיָדִי לְפוֹרְטָה, אֲפִילוּ שָׁוֶה פְרוּטָה:

מִהֲרָה וְשָׁאֲלָה מִשְּׁכֵנִים, מַלְבּוּשִׁים נָאִים מְתֻקָּנִים, **B** נִלְבַּשׁ וְהִשְׁלִיךְ יְהָבוֹ, עַל יי אֲשֶׁר אֲהֵבוֹ, סָחוּ יְלָדָיו בְּפִלּוּלָם, אַל יָשֹׁב דַּךְ נִכְלָם:

עָבַר בַּשּׁוּק בְּסִבְרָתוֹ, וְהִנֵּה אֵלִיָּהוּ הַנָּבִיא לִקְרָאתוֹ, פָּץ לוֹ הַמְבַשֵּׂר, בֶּאֱמֶת הַיּוֹם תִּתְעַשֵּׁר,

C צַוֵּנִי בְּכָל כְּבוֹדֶךָ, כִּי הִנְנִי עַבְדֶּךָ, קְרָא לְמִי בְדַעְתּוֹ, קְנוֹת עֶבֶד אֵין כְּמוֹתוֹ, רָחַשׁ אֵיךְ יְשַׁנֶּה דִינוֹ, עֶבֶד לִמְכּוֹר אֶת אֲדוֹנוֹ, שָׁת לוֹ חָכְמָתוֹ בְּקִרְבּוֹ, וְהֶחֱזִיק בּוֹ כְּמוֹ רַבּוֹ:

D תַּגָּר קְנָאוֹ בָּאַהֲבִים, בִּשְׁמוֹנֶה מֵאוֹת אֶלֶף זְהוּבִים, תָּבְעוּ מַה מְּלַאכְתֶּךָ, אִם בְּבִנְיָן חָכְמָתֶךָ, **B** תַּכְלִית טְרַקְלִין וּפַלְטְרִין, הֲרֵי אַתָּה בֶּן חוֹרִין:

יוֹם רִאשׁוֹן בְּמִפְעָלִים, פָּעַל עִם פּוֹעֲלִים, שִׁוַּע

19

8. ISH CHOSID HOYOH

אִישׁ חָסִיד הָיָה

Chassidei Breslov

A Andante

Ish cho-sid ho-yoh, b'li mo-zoin u-mich'-yoh, b'-vei-soi `oi-seik mi-
lei-voish, v'-ein be-ged li-l'-boish, goi - - nein ba-cha-shu-voh i-
shoh v'-gam b'-vo-nim cha-mi-shoh.

B
Di - b'roh
soiroh mo -
loi ho' - i-shoh, yoi - seir ein l'his'-yo-ashoh, b'-
tsoso ki yo-ga`-to, mah noi-chal mei-`a-toh.

ha-mib'-li le-chem le'-e choil, b'-
Zo - - hir k'-var no-shuk,

1. ei-rum uv'-choi-ser koil,
2. v'-ha-loi sei-tsei la-shuk.

C
Cha-nun v'-ra-chum bim'-roi-mov, ulai yig'-m'-
`atst b'-da-`as u-v'-choch-moh, `a-tso-seich
lei-nu b'-ra-cha-mov, toiv l'-koi-vov macha-
b'li l'-has-ki-moh, k'-tsei-si l'-voishes v'-lich'-li-

20

Am   Am   Dm   1. Am   E7

48

seh,   r' - tsoin   y' - rei - ov   ya - `a - seh.

moh,   mi - b'li   ch' - sus v' - sal' - - - - - - - Yo -

2. Am   E   **D** Am   Am E Am   Am   Am

53

moh.   L' - ein b' - yo - di l' - foir - toh, a - fi - lu

Dm   Am   E   Am   Am   E Am

60

sho - veh f'ru - - - toh. Mi - ha - roh v' - sho - 'a - loh mi - sh'chei -

Am   Am   Eaug E7 Am   E Am

66

nim,   mal - bu - shim no - im m' - su - ko - nim.

midnight, "Answer me, Miracle-worker! I took the initiative to be sold as a slave for Your glory, not for mine.

"Creator and Master of the universe, complete this building. May Your compassion be aroused by my entreaty, for my intention was good."

Angels of mercy from His dwelling then began to build it. There were so many builders of the palace that the entire project was completed. The merchant was overjoyed when he saw that it was finished, complete with fine towers, befitting the finest builders.

"Remember now what you promised yesterday; free me totally and absolutely, as you spoke regarding setting free." [The merchant] was honest and kept his word, and [Eliyohu], the man of truth, flew off.

בַּחֲצִי הַלַּיְלָה, עֲנֵנִי נוֹרָא עֲלִילָה, יְזַמְתִּי וְנִמְכַּרְתִּי לְהַעֲבִידִי, לִכְבוֹדְךָ וְלֹא לִכְבוֹדִי:

C בּוֹרֵא עוֹלָם בְּקִנְיָן, הַשְׁלֵם זֶה הַבִּנְיָן, רַחֲמֶיךָ יִכְמְרוּ בַּחֲנִינָתִי, כִּי לְטוֹבָה כַּוָּנָתִי,

מַלְאֲכֵי רַחֲמִים מִמְּעוֹנָתוֹ, אָז הֵחֵלּוּ לִבְנוֹתוֹ: רַבּוּ בְּנֵי הַמְּלוּכָה, וַתִּשְׁלַם כָּל הַמְּלָאכָה, **D** דָּץ הַסּוֹחֵר בִּרְאוֹתוֹ כִּי נִגְמְרָה מְלַאכְתּוֹ, כְּלוּלַת מִגְדָּלִים נָאִים, לְפִי עִנְיַן הַבַּנָּאִים:

B יִזָּכֶר לְךָ עַתָּה, אֶתְמוֹל אֲשֶׁר דִּבַּרְתָּ, חָפְשֵׁנִי בְּוַדַּאי וּבִבְרֵירוּת, כְּנַמְתָּ לְעִנְיַן שִׁחֲרוּר, זֶה קִיְּמוֹ בֶּאֱמֶת, (זֶה קִיְּמוֹ בֶּאֱמֶת, זֶה קִיְּמוֹ בֶּאֱמֶת,) וּפָרַח לוֹ אִישׁ הָאֱמֶת:

8. Ish Chosid Hoyoh

The text for this *zemer* is found in the Machzor Vitry with some variants, and the source of the story on which it is based is found in the *Sipurei Ma'asios* of Rav Nissim Ga'on. The composer ordered the text according to the *alef-beis* and signed his name, Yishai Bar Mordechai Chazak, in the initial letters of the remaining lines.

The *niggun* was sung in Uman and has also been heard among chassidim of Karlin, Boyan and Rizhin. It is a lovely four-part waltz. The form is: || A | |: B :||: C :|| D ||.

9. OMAR HASHEM L'YA`AKOIV 1

אָמַר ה' לְיַעֲקֹב א'

R' Yisroel Ba'al Shem Tov

A — O - mar Ha-Shem l' - - Ya`a-koiv, al ti - ro `av-di Ya-`a-koiv.

Bo - char Ha-Shem b' - - Ya`a-koiv, al ti - ro `av-di Ya-`a-koiv.

B — Go-al Ha-Shem es Ya`a-koiv, al ti - ro `av-di Ya-`a-koiv.

Do - rach koi - chav mi-Ya`a-koiv, al ti - ro `av-di Ya-`a-koiv.

C — Ha - bo - im yash - reish Ya`a-koiv, al ti - ro `av-di Ya-`a-koiv.

V' - - yeird mi - - Ya`a-koiv, al ti - ro `av-di Ya-`a-koiv.

22

B

48 | A | D | A | Bm | A | D

Z' - choir zois l' - Ya`a - koiv, al

54 | A | Bm | A | D | A | Bm

ti - ro `av - di Ya - `a - koiv. Ched - vas y' - shu - `ois Ya - `a -

60 | A | Bm | Em7 | A7 | D

koiv, al ti - ro `av - di Ya - `a - koiv.

Omar Hashem L'Ya'akoiv

God spoke to Ya'akoiv—fear not, My servant Ya'akoiv.

God chose Ya'akoiv—fear not, My servant Ya'akoiv.

God redeemed Ya'akoiv—fear not, My servant Ya'akoiv.

A star has risen from Ya'akoiv—fear not, My servant Ya'akoiv.

Those who come will find their roots in Ya'akoiv—fear not, My servant Ya'akoiv.

A ruler will come from Ya'akoiv—fear not, My servant Ya'akoiv.

Remind Ya'akoiv of this—fear not, My servant Ya'akoiv.

Delightful redemption will come to Ya'akoiv—fear not, My servant Ya'akoiv.

Ya'akoiv, your tents are good—fear not, My servant Ya'akoiv.

They will teach Your laws to Ya'akoiv—fear not, My servant Ya'akoiv.

For there is no necromancy with Ya'akoiv—fear not, My servant Ya'akoiv.

He sees no sin in Ya'akoiv—fear not, My servant Ya'akoiv.

אָמַר ה׳ ליעקב

אָמַר יי לְיַעֲקֹב אַל תִּירָא עַבְדִּי יַעֲקֹב:

בָּחַר יי בְּיַעֲקֹב אַל תִּירָא עַבְדִּי יַעֲקֹב:

גָּאַל יי אֶת יַעֲקֹב אַל תִּירָא עַבְדִּי יַעֲקֹב:

דָּרַךְ כּוֹכָב מִיַּעֲקֹב אַל תִּירָא עַבְדֵי יַעֲקֹב:

הַבָּאִים יַשְׁרֵשׁ יַעֲקֹב אַל תִּירָא עַבְדִּי יַעֲקֹב:

וְיֵרְדְּ מִיַּעֲקֹב אַל תִּירָא עַבְדִּי יַעֲקֹב:

זְכֹר זֹאת לְיַעֲקֹב אַל תִּירָא עַבְדִּי יַעֲקֹב:

חֶדְוַת יְשׁוּעוֹת יַעֲקֹב אַל תִּירָא עַבְדִּי יַעֲקֹב:

A טֹבוּ אֹהָלֶיךָ יַעֲקֹב אַל תִּירָא עַבְדִּי יַעֲקֹב:

יוֹרוּ מִשְׁפָּטֶיךָ לְיַעֲקֹב אַל תִּירָא עַבְדִּי יַעֲקֹב:

B כִּי לֹא נַחַשׁ בְּיַעֲקֹב אַל תִּירָא עַבְדִּי יַעֲקֹב:

לֹא הִבִּיט אָוֶן בְּיַעֲקֹב אַל תִּירָא עַבְדִּי יַעֲקֹב:

<table>
<tr><td>Who can count the masses of Ya'akoiv—fear not, My servant Ya'akoiv.</td><td dir="rtl">מִי מָנָה עֲפַר יַעֲקֹב אַל תִּירָא עַבְדִּי יַעֲקֹב: C</td></tr>
<tr><td>God gave an oath to Ya'akoiv—fear not, My servant Ya'akoiv.</td><td dir="rtl">נִשְׁבַּע יי לְיַעֲקֹב אַל תִּירָא עַבְדִּי יַעֲקֹב:</td></tr>
<tr><td>Forgive the sin of Ya'akoiv—fear not, My servant Ya'akoiv.</td><td dir="rtl">סְלַח נָא לַעֲוֹן יַעֲקֹב אַל תִּירָא עַבְדִּי יַעֲקֹב: B</td></tr>
<tr><td>Now, release those of Ya'akoiv in captivity—fear not, My servant Ya'akoiv.</td><td dir="rtl">עַתָּה הָשֵׁב שְׁבוּת יַעֲקֹב אַל תִּירָא עַבְדִּי יַעֲקֹב:</td></tr>
<tr><td>God redeemed Ya'akoiv—fear not, My servant Ya'akoiv.</td><td dir="rtl">פָּדָה יי אֶת יַעֲקֹב אַל תִּירָא עַבְדִּי יַעֲקֹב: A</td></tr>
<tr><td>Command the salvation of Ya'akoiv—fear not, My servant Ya'akoiv.</td><td dir="rtl">צַוֵּה יְשׁוּעוֹת יַעֲקֹב אַל תִּירָא עַבְדִּי יַעֲקֹב:</td></tr>
<tr><td>The voice is the voice of Ya'akoiv—fear not, My servant Ya'akoiv.</td><td dir="rtl">קוֹל קוֹל יַעֲקֹב אַל תִּירָא עַבְדִּי יַעֲקֹב: B</td></tr>
<tr><td>Sing to and gladden Ya'akoiv—fear not, My servant Ya'akoiv.</td><td dir="rtl">רָנִּי וְשִׂמְחִי לְיַעֲקֹב אַל תִּירָא עַבְדִּי יַעֲקֹב:</td></tr>
<tr><td>God will return Yaakov's pride—fear not, My servant Ya'akoiv.</td><td dir="rtl">שָׁב יי אֶת שְׁבוּת יַעֲקֹב אַל תִּירָא עַבְדִּי יַעֲקֹב:</td></tr>
<tr><td>Give truth to Ya'akoiv—fear not, My servant Ya'akoiv.</td><td dir="rtl">תִּתֵּן אֱמֶת לְיַעֲקֹב אַל תִּירָא עַבְדִּי יַעֲקֹב:</td></tr>
</table>

9. Omar HaShem L'Ya'akoiv 1

Verses of this *zemer* are taken from verses in the Torah concerning Jacob our patriarch, who symbolizes the Jewish people, Israel. The initial letters of the verses follow the *alef-beis*.

The *niggun*, sung exclusively by Breslovers, is attributed to none other than the holy Ba'al Shem Tov, Rebbe Nachman's great-grandfather, and was originally set to the text *"Hodu L'HaShem Ki Tov, Ki L'olom Chasdo."* The story that was passed down with the *niggun* tells of how, through the Ba'al Shem Tov, a salvation came about for the Jewish community of Istanbul when the Ba'al Shem Tov stopped there for Pesach during his attempted but ultimately unsuccessful trip to the Holy Land. He was sitting on his hotel balcony singing this *niggun* as the emissaries of the Jewish community passed the hotel on their way to try to annul the evil decree.

The *niggun* is in three parts and the form is || A | B | C | B ||. It is sung in a march tempo.

10. OMAR HASHEM L'YA`AKOIV 2

אָמַר ה' לְיַעֲקֹב ב'

Chassidei Breslov

Andante Maestoso

10. Omar HaShem L'Ya'akoiv 2

Some Breslover chassidim sing this *niggun* to the whole text of the *zemer*, while others employ it only for the last two lines. The refrain in Yiddish, "Yo Tatte Yo..." was heard among various chassidim in the Ukraine. Each verse ends with the refrain, "*al tiro avdi Ya'akoiv*" (fear not, My servant Ya'akoiv.) The concluding line in Yiddish is our answer to God: "We fear no one but You alone."

11. NIGGUN SIMCHOH

נִיגוּן שִׂמְחָה

Allegro

Chassidei Breslov

Lai lai lai   lai lai lai   lai la la lai lai   lai lai   lai lai...

Fine

D.S. al Fine

26

11. Niggun Simchoh

Many *niggunim* without words have come into the Breslover repertoire, some original and some brought from outside sources. During the *Melave Malka* celebration, there will often be a circle-dance, during which various *niggunim* will be sung or played. This *niggun,* according to some, was sung in Uman before the Communists came to power. Others attribute it to R' Shloimo Wechsler, who became a Breslover chassid in the 1940s and composed beautiful *niggunim.*

It is a three-part song in major whose form is || A A | B B | C C | B B ||.

12. HaMavdil

This *niggut* was written by Yitzchok HaKoton (יצחק הקטן), who signed his name in the initial letters of verses 2-9. Rabbi Mordechai ben Hillel (1250-1298), known as "The Mordechai," mentions in his commentary to tractate *Yoma* that this *piyut* was sung in the synagogue at the conclusion of Yom Kippur.

It is now sung after Havdalah in many congregations. The composer of the music is not known, but it was sung in Uman by Breslover chassidim for over a hundred years. "HaMavdil" is a two-part *niggun* in Dorian mode. Breslover chassidim, known in the past as "*viduinikim*" (ones who are always confessing their sins as part of their *hisbodedus,* conversing with God), add emphasis through repetition to phrases such as "*p'sach li sha'ar ham'nutal*" (open the Heavenly gate for me), "*ashavei'a*" (I cry out), "*taheir tinuf ma'asai*" (purify the filth of my deeds), and "*s'lach no*" (please forgive). These unique repetitions turn the *piyut* into a very potent prayer.

12. HAMAVDIL

הַמַּבְדִּיל

Nusach of R' Nachman Burstein

Moderato

Chassidei Breslov

A D Em D Em D A D G D A D

Ha - mav - dil bein koi - desh l' - choil, cha - toi - sei - nu Hu yim - choil.
Yoim po - noh k' - tseil toimer, e - k'ro lo - Keil olai goi - meir.

Em Am C D Em Am

Zar - `ei - nu v'-chas - pei - nu yar - beh yar - beh ka - choil, zar - `ei - nu v'-chas - pei - nu
O - mar shoi - meir o - so boi - ker, o - mar shoi - meir

A7 D G B7 1. Em

yar - beh yar - beh ka - choil, v'-cha-koi-cho-vim ba - loy - loh.
o - - so boi - ker, o - so boi - ker v' - gam loy - - -

2. Em **B** C Em Am D

loh.
Tsid - kos - cho k' - Har To - voir,

C D Em Am A7 D Em

al cha - to - ai `o - voir ta - `a - voir, al cha - to' - ai

Am D C D Em Am C D

al cha - to' - ai al cha - to' - ai `o - voir ta - `a - voir,

Em Am Em D Em Bm F#7 Bm

k' - yoim es - moil ki ya - `a - voir, v'-ash - mu - roh va - loy - loh.

28

HaMavdil

המבדיל

זה הזמר שם המחבר יצחק הקטן:

May the One Who distinguishes between sacred and profane forgive our sins. May He multiply our offspring and our wealth like the sand and like the stars of night.

הַמַּבְדִּיל בֵּין קֹדֶשׁ לְחוֹל, חַטֹּאתֵינוּ הוּא יִמְחוֹל. זַרְעֵנוּ וְכַסְפֵּנוּ יַרְבֶּה כַּחוֹל. וְכַכּוֹכָבִים בַּלָּיְלָה:

As the day passes like the shade of the palm tree, I call to God to fulfill what He promised me. The Guardian said, "Dawn has come [for the righteous], and night [for the wicked]."

יוֹם פָּנָה כְּצֵל תֹּמֶר, אֶקְרָא לָאֵל עָלַי גּוֹמֵר, אָמַר שׁוֹמֵר, אָתָא בֹקֶר וְגַם לָיְלָה:

Your righteousness is as great as Mount Tabor. Treat my sins as something past, like the evening watch.

צִדְקָתְךָ כְּהַר תָּבוֹר, עַל חֲטָאַי עָבוֹר תַּעֲבוֹר, כְּיוֹם אֶתְמוֹל כִּי יַעֲבוֹר, וְאַשְׁמוּרָה בַלָּיְלָה:

The time for my rest has passed—who will grant me rest?! I am weary with groaning; every night I drench my bed with tears.

🅐 חָלְפָה עוֹנַת מִנְחָתִי, מִי יִתֵּן מְנוּחָתִי, יָגַעְתִּי בְאַנְחָתִי, אַשְׂחֶה בְכָל לַיְלָה:

May my prayers not be refused; open the Heavenly gate for me, for the hair of my head is drenched with tears like dew, my locks with tears like the rain of night.

🅑 קוֹלִי בַּל יִנְטָל, פְּתַח לִי שַׁעַר הַמְּנֻטָּל, שֶׁרֹאשִׁי נִמְלָא טָל, קְוֻצּוֹתַי רְסִיסֵי לָיְלָה:

Be receptive, Awesome and Fearsome One. I cry out, "Grant redemption," at dusk, in the evening, in the dark hours of night.

🅑 הֵעָתֵר נוֹרָא וְאָיוֹם, אֲשַׁוֵּעַ תְּנָה פִדְיוֹם, בְּנֶשֶׁף בְּעֶרֶב יוֹם, בְּאִישׁוֹן לָיְלָה:

I called to You, O God, "Save me! Show me the path in life. End my poverty before the day is over."

🅐 קְרָאתִיךָ יָהּ הוֹשִׁיעֵנִי, אֹרַח חַיִּים תּוֹדִיעֵנִי, מִדַּלּוּת תְּבַצְּעֵנִי, מִיּוֹם וְעַד לָיְלָה:

Purify the filth of my deeds, lest those who torment me ask where is God my Maker, who gives reason for song at night?

🅐 טַהֵר נָא מַעֲשַׂי, פֶּן יֹאמְרוּ מַכְעִיסַי, אַיֵּה נָא אֱלוֹהַּ עֹשָׂי, הַנּוֹתֵן זְמִירוֹת בַּלָּיְלָה:

In Your hands we are like clay; please forgive our minor and major sins. Day in and day out, and every night we will speak Your praises.

🅑 נַחְנוּ בְיָדְךָ כַּחֹמֶר, סְלַח נָא עַל קַל וָחֹמֶר, יוֹם לְיוֹם יַבִּיעַ אֹמֶר, וְלַיְלָה לְלָיְלָה:

May the One Who distinguishes...

🅐 המבדיל...

13. ELIYOHU HANOVI

אֵלִיָּהוּ הַנָּבִיא

Nusach of R' Moishe Bienenstock

Chassidei Breslov

Moderato

E - li - yo - hu Ha - no - vi E - li - yo - hu Ha - Tish - bi E - li-
yo - hu Ha - Gi - lo - di, E - li - yo - hu Ha - no - vi E - li-yo-hu Ha - Tish - bi E - li-
yo - hu Ha - Gi - lo - di, bim - hei - roh yo - voi yo - voi
yo - voi ei - lei - nu `im Mo - shi - ach ben Do - vid.  `im Mo - shi - ach ben Do-

Fine

vid. Ish a - sher ki - nei l'sheim ho - Keil, ish bu - sar sho - loim `al yad Y"-ku - si -
Ish doi - rois shneim osor ro - u ei - nov ish hani - k'ro ba`al  sei - `or b' - si - mo-

eil, ish gosh va - y'-cha-peir `al b' - nei Yis-ro' - eil.
nov, ish v'ei - zoir `oir o - zur b' - mos' - nov.

D.C. al Fine

30

Eliyohu HaNavi

Eliyohu the prophet, Eliyohu the Tishbite, Eliyohu of Gilead—may he quickly come to us with the Moshiach, the son of David.

The man who was zealous for the name of God; the man who was assured peace by God's messenger of hope; the man who stepped forth and atoned for the Children of Israel. *Eliyohu the prophet…*

The man whose eyes saw twelve generations; the man called "hairy one" because of his appearance; the man with a leather belt girding his loins. *Eliyohu the prophet…*

The man who raged against the sun worshipers; the man who hurriedly swore that there would be no rain from Heaven; the man who withheld dew and rain for three years. *Eliyohu the prophet…*

The man who went forth to find tranquility for his soul; the man who was nourished by ravens, who did not die and go to the grave; the man on whose behalf jug and jar were blessed. *Eliyohu the prophet…*

The man whose moral teachings were heeded by those yearning; the man answered with fire from the Heavens above; the man after whom they repeated, "The Lord is God!" *Eliyohu the prophet…*

The man designated to be sent from the Heavens; the man appointed over all good tidings; the man who is the trustworthy agent to reconcile children with parents. *Eliyohu the prophet…*

The man who proclaimed in splendor, "I acted zealously for the sake of God"; the man who rode fiery horses in a whirlwind; the man who never tasted death or burial. *Eliyohu the prophet…*

The man who is also called "the Tishbite," make us successful in Torah through him; let us soon hear good tidings from his mouth; bring us forth from darkness to light. *Eliyohu the prophet…*

אליהו הנביא

אֵלִיָּהוּ הַנָּבִיא אֵלִיָּהוּ הַתִּשְׁבִּי אֵלִיָּהוּ הַגִּלְעָדִי בִּמְהֵרָה יָבֹא אֵלֵינוּ עִם מָשִׁיחַ בֶּן דָּוִד:

אִישׁ אֲשֶׁר קִנֵּא לְשֵׁם הָאֵל, אִישׁ בֻּשַּׂר שָׁלוֹם עַל יַד יְקוּתִיאֵל, אִישׁ גָּשׁ וַיְכַפֵּר עַל בְּנֵי יִשְׂרָאֵל: אליהו

אִישׁ דּוֹרוֹת שְׁנֵים עָשָׂר רָאוּ עֵינָיו, אִישׁ הַנִּקְרָא בַּעַל שֵׂעָר בְּסִמָּנָיו, אִישׁ וְאֵזוֹר עוֹר אָזוּר בְּמָתְנָיו: אליהו

אִישׁ זָעַף עַל עוֹבְדֵי חַמָּנִים, אִישׁ חָשׁ וְנִשְׁבַּע מִהְיוֹת גִּשְׁמֵי מְעוֹנִים, אִישׁ טַל וּמָטָר עָצַר שָׁלֹשׁ שָׁנִים: אליהו

אִישׁ יָצָא לִמְצֹא לְנַפְשׁוֹ נַחַת, אִישׁ כִּלְכְּלוּהוּ הָעוֹרְבִים וְלֹא מֵת לַשַּׁחַת, אִישׁ לְמַעֲנוֹ נִתְבָּרְכוּ כַּד וְצַפַּחַת: אליהו

אִישׁ מוּסָרָיו הִקְשִׁיבוּ כְמֵהִים, אִישׁ נַעֲנָה בָּאֵשׁ מִשְּׁמֵי גְבוֹהִים, אִישׁ סָחוּ אַחֲרָיו יי הוּא הָאֱלֹהִים: אליהו

אִישׁ עָתִיד לְהִשְׁתַּלֵּחַ מִשְּׁמֵי עֲרָבוֹת, אִישׁ פָּקִיד עַל כָּל בְּשׂוֹרוֹת טוֹבוֹת, אִישׁ צִיר נֶאֱמָן לְהָשִׁיב לֵב בָּנִים עַל אָבוֹת: אליהו

אִישׁ קָרָא קַנֹּא קִנֵּאתִי לַיהֹוָה בְּתִפְאָרָה, אִישׁ רָכַב עַל סוּסֵי אֵשׁ בִּסְעָרָה, אִישׁ שֶׁלֹּא טָעַם טַעַם מִיתָה וּקְבוּרָה: אליהו

אִישׁ תִּשְׁבִּי עַל שְׁמוֹ נִקְרָא, תַּצְלִיחֵנוּ עַל יָדוֹ בַּתּוֹרָה, תַּשְׁמִיעֵנוּ מִפִּיו בְּשׂוֹרָה טוֹבָה בִּמְהֵרָה, תּוֹצִיאֵנוּ מֵאֲפֵלָה לְאוֹרָה: אליהו

13. Eliyohu HaNovi

The text is composed of biblical references to the qualities and events in the life of of Elijah the Prophet. The verses trace the *alef-beis* in the initial letter of the word following the word *"Ish."*

The music is the Breslover version of the universally popular song.

Ashrei Mi SheRo'oh

Happy is he who has seen his face in a dream; happy is the one who has greeted him with "Shalom," and to whom he responded, "Shalom." May God bless His people with peace. *Eliyohu the prophet...*

As it is written: "Behold, I will send to you Eliyohu the prophet before the coming of the awesome, fearful day of the Lord. He shall reconcile parents with children and children with their parents." *Eliyohu the prophet...*

אשרי מי שראה

אַשְׁרֵי מִי שֶׁרָאָה פָּנָיו בַּחֲלוֹם, אַשְׁרֵי מִי שֶׁנָּתַן לוֹ שָׁלוֹם וְהֶחֱזִיר לוֹ שָׁלוֹם. יי יְבָרֵךְ אֶת עַמּוֹ בַשָׁלוֹם: אליהו

כַּכָּתוּב הִנֵּה אָנֹכִי שֹׁלֵחַ לָכֶם אֶת אֵלִיָּה הַנָּבִיא לִפְנֵי בֹּא יוֹם יי הַגָּדוֹל וְהַנּוֹרָא: וְהֵשִׁיב לֵב אָבוֹת עַל בָּנִים וְלֵב בָּנִים עַל אֲבוֹתָם: אליהו

14. Ashrei Mi SheRo'oh 1

The last two verses of the previous *zemer* are sung to a separate *niggun* in Breslov.

This *niggun* was brought to Uman by Reb Bentsiyoin Apter. Some say it had been previously sung in a secular theatrical production. It is a lovely, two-part waltz.

32

14. ASHREI MI SHE'RO'OH 1

אַשְׁרֵי מִי שֶׁרָאָה א׳

Chassidei Breslov

Waltz

1. Ash - - - rei	mi she'-ro'-oh fo-nov ba-cha-	
2, 4. yo - hu Ha - no - vi,	E - li-yo - hu Ha - no -	
3. Ka - ko - suv	hinei o-noi-chi shoi-lei-ach lo-	

loim, ash-rei mi she'-no-san loi sho-loim, v'-heche-zir
vi, Eli-yo-hu Ha-Tish-bi, Eli-yo-hu
chem es Eli-yo-hu Ha-No-vi es Eli-yo-hu

loi sho-loim, Ha-Shem y'-vo-reich y'-
HaGi-lo-di, oy Bim-hei-roh yo-voi ei-lei-nu
Ha-No-vi lif-nei bo yoim Ha-Shem ha-

vo-reich es `a-moi va-sho-loim. Lai lai la la ...
`im Ma-shi-ach ben Do-vid. Bim-hei-roh yo-voi ei-
go-doil v'-ha-noi-ro. V'-hei-shiv lev o-vois `al bo-

1.

lai lai lai lai lai la la lai lai lai. Eli - - -
lei-nu `imMa-shi-ach ben Do - - - - - vid.
nim v'-leiv bo-nim `al a - voi-som.

2.

33

15. ASHREI MI SHE'RO'OH 2

אַשְׁרֵי מִי שֶׁרָאָה ב'

Chassidei Breslov

Ah la la lai la la la lai la la la lai la la la lai. Ash-rei mi ash-rei mi she'-

ro' - oh fo-nov fo-nov ba-cha-loim, ash-rei mi she'-no-san loi sho-loim, v'-

heche - zir loi sho - loim, v' - heche - zir loi sho - loim,

loim, Ha - Shem `oiz l'-`a-moi yi-tein, Ai lai lai la la la la la Ha-Shem y'-

vo - reich es `a-moi va-sho-loim. Ai Ka - - - - - -

ka - - - - - - ka - - - - - - - - -

ka - - - - - - - - ka - ka - ko - suv

Hi - nei o-noi - chi shoi-lei - ach lo-chem es E-li-yo-hu Ha-no-vi lif - nei boi yoim Ha - Shem ha - go - doil v'-ha - noi - ro. V' -

hei - shiv leiv o - vois `al bo - nim lai lai lai

lai v' - leiv bo - nim `al a - voi - som.

16. Ashrei Mi SheRo'oh 2

Another version of the last two verses of *"Eliyohu HaNovi"* is this original Breslover *niggun* sung in Uman and brought to Israel by Rav Levi Yitschok Bender. With no rigid form, this *niggun* resembles a fanfare in its majestic major tonality, with recurring motifs that are idiomatic for brass instruments.

16. PUROH DORACHTI

פּוּרָה דָּרַכְתִּי

Allegro

Chassidei Breslov

INTRO — Cm / Fm / Cm / Bb
Pu - roh do-rach-ti l'-va-di, u-mei-`a-mim ein ish i-

Eb / Eb / Bb / Eb / G
ti, v'-ed-r'-cheim b'-a-pi, v'er-m'-seim ba-cha-mo-si. V'-

Fm / G / Cm
Noi - ach mo-tso chein b'-ei - nei Ha-Shem. Vay'-

B — Eb / Bb / Eb / Eb / Cm Bb Ab
hi Do - vid l'-chol d'-ro-chov mas-kil va-Ha-Shem `i-moi.

Eb / Bb Cm / Eb Fm Cm Bb Fm / G / Cm
La la lai lai lai la la lai lai lai lai lai lai lai lai lai lai lai la la lai lai lai.

A — Cm / Fm / Cm Bb / Cm
Pu - roh do-rach-ti l'-va-di, u-mei-`a-mim ein ish i-ti, la lai lai lai la la lai lai lai lai,

Cm / Fm / Cm G7 / Cm
v'-ed-r'-cheim b'-a-pi, v'-er-m'-seim ba-cha-mo-si, la la lai lai lai la la lai lai lai.

B — Eb / Bb / Eb / Eb / G / Cm
Lai lai lai lai la la lai lai lai, lai lai lai lai lai lai. V'-

36

Puroh Dorachti

I trod the winepress alone; no one from the nations was with Me. I trod them in my anger and trampled them in my wrath (Isaiah 63:3).

And Noach found grace in God's eyes (Genesis 6:8).

And David was successful in all that he did, for God was with him (I Samuel 18:14).

פּוּרָה דָרַכְתִּי

פּוּרָה דָרַכְתִּי לְבַדִּי, וּמֵעַמִּים אֵין אִישׁ אִתִּי,
וְאֶדְרְכֵם בְּאַפִּי, וְאֶרְמְסֵם בַּחֲמָתִי:

וְנֹחַ מָצָא חֵן בְּעֵינֵי יי:

וַיְהִי דָוִד לְכָל דְּרָכָו מַשְׂכִּיל וַיהוָֹה עִמּוֹ:

15. Puroh Dorachti

This song follows the singing of "*Eliyohu HaNovi*" in Breslov. It comprises a verse from Isaiah 63:3 and other biblical verses relevant to Moitso'ei Shabbos.

The tune is sung in many chassidic communities to other words, such as "*Mitzvoh g'doiloh lihiyois b'simchoh*" (It is a great mitzvah to be joyous), or without words as a dance *niggun*.

17. A GITTE VOCH

א גוטע וואך

Chassidei Breslov

Waltz

A D ... D ... C ... D ... E min

Lai lai lai la la lai lai la la lai lai la la lai lai lai lai lai

A ... D ... A ... D ... D ... C

lai la lai, A gi-te voch, a frei-li-che voch. Lai lai lai la la lai lai la la lai lai

B min ... E min7 ... A ... D ... D

la la lai lai lai lai lai lai la lai. A gi-te voch, a frei-li-che voch.

B G ... G ... D ... D ... C

La la lai lai lai la la lai lai lai lai la la lai lai lai

A ... D ... A ... G ... G

lai la lai. A gi-te voch, a frei-li-che voch. La la lai lai lai la la

D ... B min ... E min7 ... A ... D

lai lai lai lai la la lai lai lai lai lai. A gi-te voch, a

D ... **C** F ... D ... A ... D

frei-li-che voch. *Fine* La la la la la la lai la la lai lai lai lai la la

38

lai lai lai lai la lai. A gi - te voch, a frei - li - che voch.

La la la la la la lai la la lai lai lai lai la la

lai lai lai lai la lai. A gi - te voch, a frei - li - che voch.

D.S. al Fine

A Gitte Voch

A good week, a happy week.

אַ גוטע וואָך

אַ גוטע וואָך, אַ פרייליכע וואָך:

17. A Gitte Voch

The text is simply a salutation wishing friends a good and joyous week.

The source of the tune is unknown, but has been sung in Breslov for about a century. It is a three-part, waltz-like *niggun* in major with the form: || A | B | C | B ||.

18. V'Harikoisi Lochem B'rochoh

The first line of text is a quote from Malachi 3:10, and the last line is the comment of the Gemora (*Ta'anis* 9a) on this verse.

The *niggun* is the Breslover version of a tune sung slightly differently by other chassidic groups. In Breslov, some replace the words "*kol hatsadikim hanikro'im chai*" alternately with "*Rabbeinu HaKodoish ish tsadik chai,*" referring to Rebbe Nachman, and/or "*HaTanna ho'Eloiki Rabbi Shim'on bar Yochai.*"

18. V'HARIKOISI LOCHEM BROCHOH

וַהֲרִיקֹתִי לָכֶם בְּרָכָה

Chassidei Breslov

Allegro

Lyrics under music (verse lines):

V'-ha-ri-koi-si lo-chem b'ro-choh `ad b'-li dai, bi-

z'chus kol ha-tsa-di-kim ha-ni-k'ro-im chai. Ad she-
ha-Tanno ho'e-loiki Rabbi Shim-`on Bar Yoi-choi.
Ra-beinu Ha-ko-doish ish tsa-dik chai.

yiv - lu sif - soi-sei-chem mi - loi-mar

dai dai dai. Ad she-yiv - lu sif - soi-

sei - chem mi - loi-mar dai dai dai. *D.C.*

V'Harikoisi Lochem B'rochoh

I will pour out blessing for you without limit.

In the merit of *all the righteous, who are called living.

Till our lips dry up from saying, "Enough."

* The Godly Tanna, Rabbi Shimon Bar Yochoi

* Our holy Rebbe, a living righteous man

וַהֲרִיקֹתִי לָכֶם בְּרָכָה

"וַהֲרִיקֹתִי לָכֶם בְּרָכָה עַד־בְּלִי־דָי:" (מלאכי ג:י)

בִּזְכוּת *כָּל הַצַּדִּקִים הַנִּקְרָאִים חַי

"עַד שֶׁיִּבְלוּ שִׂפְתוֹתֵיכֶם, מִלּוֹמַר דַּי דַּי דָי:"
(תענית ט.)

*הַתַּנָּא הָאֱלֹקִי רַבִּי שִׁמְעוֹן בַּר יוֹחַי

*רַבֵּינוּ הַקָּדוֹשׁ אִישׁ צַדִּיק חַי

19. DOVID MELECH YISROEL

דָּוִד מֶלֶךְ יִשְׂרָאֵל

Chassidei Breslov

March

Do-vid me-lech me-lech Yis-ro-el chai chai v'-ka-yom, Do-vid me-lech

me-lech Yis-ro-el chai chai v'-ka-yom, Do - vid me-lech Yis-ro-

el chai chai chai v'-ka-yom, Do-vid me-lech

me-lech Yis-ro-el chai chai v'-ka-yom, Do-vid me-lech me-lech Yis-ro-el

chai chai v'-ka-yom.

David Melech Yisroel

David, King of Israel, lives and endures.

דָּוִד מֶלֶךְ יִשְׂרָאֵל
דָּוִד מֶלֶךְ יִשְׂרָאֵל חַי וְקַיָּם:

19. Dovid Melech Yisroel

The words are found in the Gemora (*Rosh Hashanah* 25a) and in the *siddur* at *Kiddush Levonoh*, which is most often recited on Moitso'ei Shabbos.

The *niggun* was sung at the end of the Moitso'ei Shabbos *zmiros* and also in Meron by Breslover chassidim who often visited the grave of Rabbi Shimon bar Yochai. It is a two-part song similar to the popular song of the same text.

INDEX OF SONG TITLES

רשימת ניגונים

BRESLOV MUSIC TRANSCRIPTIONS AND RECORDINGS

SONGBOOKS

The traditional music of Chassidei Breslov is being published by the Breslov Research Institute. Collected and transcribed by Ben Zion Solomon, each volume includes accompanying song text, simple chords, original Hebrew text, English translation, transliteration of the Hebrew text into phonetic English, commentary and historical information on each song.

The Breslov Songbook Volume 1 - Azameir BiSh'vochin contains 21 songs from the Friday Evening synagogue songs and *zmiros* of the Evening Meal.

The Breslov Songbook Volume 2 - Asadeir LiS'udoso contains 27 pieces, covering the Shabbos Morning synagogue songs, Morning Meal *zmiros*, and *zemiros* of the Third Meal.

The Breslov Songbook Volume 3 – B'Moitso'ei Yoim M'nuchoh contains 19 songs from the Moitso'ei Shabbos *zmiros*.

RECORDINGS

SHABBOS

The Breslov Research Institute is producing an extensive recorded series documenting the entire repertoire with authenticity and accompanying notes, complementing the Breslov Songbook series. The musical production for the series is by Ben Zion Solomon.

1. AZAMER BISH'VOCHIN (BRM-D 101) - Melodies for Shabbos Evening. (Arranged by Ben Zion Solomon, sung by Rabbi Moshe Bienenstock, Rabbi Nachman Burstein, accompanied by chorus and orchestra.)

2. ME'EYN OLOM HABO (BRM-D 102) - Melodies for the Shabbos Evening Meal and Shabbos Morning Prayers. (Arranged by Ben Zion Solomon and Yisroel Edelson, sung by Rabbi Moshe Bienenstock, with Ben Zion Solomon and sons, accompanied by chorus and orchestra.)

3. ASADEIR LIS'UDOSO (BRM-D 105) - *Zmiros* for the Shabbos Morning Meal. (Arranged and sung by Ben Zion Solomon and sons, with Joel Eckhardt, accompanied by chorus and orchestra.)

4. B'NEI HEICHOLO (BRM-D 106) - *Zmiros* for the Third Meal of Shabbos. (Arranged by Yisroel Edelson, sung by Rabbi Moshe Bienenstock and Joel Eckhardt, accompanied by chorus and orchestra.)

5. B'MOITSO'EI YOIM M'NUCHOH (BRM-D 109) - The Moitso'ei Shabbos *zmiros*. (Arranged by Ben Zion Solomon, sung by Rabbi Moshe Bienenstock and Ben Zion Solomon, sons and grandsons, with instrumental ensemble.)

SIMCHOH

6. ASHREINU (BRM-D 103) - An assortment of choice Breslover *niggunim*. (Arranged by

Ben Zion Solomon and Yisroel Edelson, sung by Rabbi Nachman Burstein, accompanied by chorus and orchestra.)

7. P'LIOH (BRM-D 104) - More choice Breslover *niggunim*. (Arranged by Leib Ya'acov Rigler, sung by Rabbi Moshe Bienenstock, accompanied by chorus and orchestra.)

8. KOCHVEI BOKER (BRM-D 108) Still more choice Breslover *niggunim*. (Arranged by Leib Ya'acov Rigler, sung by Rabbi Moshe Bienenstock, accompanied by chorus and orchestra.)

MUSICAL INDEX

מפתח מוסיקלי

1 - 2. B'Moitso'ei Yoim M'nuchoh

Adagio

B'-Moi - tso - ei yoim m'nu - choh ham'-tsei l'am'-cho r' - vo-choh, shlach

3. Chadeish S'soini

Allegro

Cha-deish s'-soi - ni Keil noh v'-ho-vi es Ei-li-yo-hu ha-no-vi,

4. Ogil V'Esmach

Moderato

O - gil V'-Es-mach bil' - vo-vi, bir'-oi-si ki mei-oy' - vi to-riv ri-vi,

5. Eloikim Yis'odeinu

Moderato

E - loi-kim yis-'o-dei-nu b'-ro-choh bim'-oi-dei-nu, v'ze-ved toiv yiz

6. Keili Chish

Moderato

Kei-li chish goi-'a-li `av'-d'-cho yas'-ki-li m'va-ser toiv Kei-li es Eli -

7. Adir Oyoim V'Noiro

Adagio

A-dir o-yoim v' - noi-ro, ba-tsar li l'-cho e-k'ro, Ha -

8. Ish Chosid Hoyoh

Andante

Ish cho-sid ho - yo, b'li mo-zoin u-mich' - yoh, b'-vei-soi `oi-seik mi -

9. Omar HaShem L'Ya'akoiv 1

Moderato   R' Yisroel Ba'al Shem Tov

O - mar Ha - Shem l' - - Ya`a-koiv Al ti - ro

10. Omar HaShem L'Ya'akoiv 2

Andante Maestoso

Shov Ha-Shem es sh'vus Ya`a - koiv, Yo Tat-te yo, yo Fut-ter yo,

11. Niggun Simchoh

Allegro

Lai lai lai lai lai lai lai la la lai lai lai lai lai lai...

12. HaMavdil

Moderato

Ha - mav-dil bein koi-desh l'-choil, cha-toi-sei-nu Hu yim'-choil.

13. Eliyohu HaNovi

Moderato

E-li-yo-hu Ha-no-vi E-li-yo-hu Ha-Tish-bi E - li -

14. Ashrei Mi SheRo'oh 1

Waltz

Ash' - - rei mi she'-ro'-oh fo-nov ba-cha -

15. Ashrei Mi SheRo'oh 2

March

Ah la la lai la la lai la la lai la la la lai. Ash'-rei mi Ash'-rei mi she' -

16. Puroh Dorachti

Allegro

Pu - roh do-rach-ti l'-va-di, u-mei-`a-mim ein ish i -

17. A Gitte Voch

Waltz

Lai lai lai la la lai lai la la lai lai la la lai lai lai lai lai

18. V'Harikoisi Lochem B'rochoh

Allegro

V'-ha-ri-koi-si lo-chem b'ro - choh `ad b'-li dai, Bi-

19. Dovid Melech Yisroel

March

Do-vid me-lech me-lech Yis-ro'-el chai chai v'-ka-yom, Do-vid me-lech

www.ingramcontent.com/pod-product-compliance
Lightning Source LLC
Chambersburg PA
CBHW081152040426
42445CB00015B/1852